The Teen Entrepreneur Playbook

Unlock the Secrets of Small Business Success for Young Adults

M. A. Gallant

Etheria Publishing

Cover art by Melissa Gallant

Contents

Introduction

I N A WORLD BRIMMING with opportunities, it's not uncommon to feel the tug of entrepreneurship from a young
age. Perhaps you feel the itch to create something of your
own and forge your path rather than follow someone else's
footsteps. The allure of entrepreneurship beckons, promising freedom, fulfillment, and the chance to make a difference
in the world. Consider this: the early bird gets the worm.
Venturing into entrepreneurship at a young age isn't just

about securing your future; it's about seizing the reins of your destiny. Imagine becoming the architect of your life, sculpting your dreams into reality with every decision you make. It's exhilarating, isn't it?

Let's not forget the power of networking. By exploring entrepreneurship early on, you're jump-starting your network. Imagine rubbing shoulders with industry titans and forging connections that could last a lifetime. The world becomes your playground, and success feels within reach.

But why stop there? As a young entrepreneur, you're not just chasing profits; you're working to fix the future. With every innovation and every idea brought to life, you're daring to be daring. The world is full of success stories. If they made it, why not you?

It's not uncommon for students to enter university with dreams of entrepreneurship, inspired by those who have gone before them. Take Steve Jobs, for example. Co-founding Apple from a garage in California, Jobs shaped the tech landscape as we know it. He defied the odds to build one of the world's largest corporations. Despite never completing college, his determination to succeed propelled him forward, proving that formal education isn't always a prerequisite for entrepreneurial greatness.

Mark Zuckerberg founded Facebook from his dorm room at Harvard. What began as a simple project became a global phenomenon, showcasing ambition and innovation. Similarly, Richard Branson's Virgin Group emerged from humble beginnings, showcasing how relentless drive and creative thinking can turn dreams into reality.

Now, you might wonder, why this book? What led you to pick it up? Maybe the traditional career path doesn't interest you. Do you yearn for something more? Or perhaps you know entrepreneurship is the right road for you. Are you full of ideas but unsure where to start?

Whatever the reason, this book holds the keys to unlocking your potential as a young entrepreneur. What can you expect? Think of this book as your shortcut to success. It's packed with actionable advice, real-world stories, and expert insights to guide your entrepreneurial journey.

With each chapter, you'll gain invaluable wisdom, empowering you to navigate the highs and lows of business ownership with confidence. Don't just take my word for it. Countless others have walked this path before you, and their testimonials speak volumes. From teen tycoons to industry icons, their stories serve as a beacon of hope, proving that with determination and drive, anything is possible.

Envision a life where you're in control, and your ideas can change the world. That's the promise of entrepreneurship, and this book is your roadmap to achieving it. If you've ever felt the burning desire to carve your path and leave your mark, trust me—this book is perfect for you. It's time to turn your dreams into reality and join the ranks of successful young entrepreneurs who dared to defy the odds.

Chapter 1
Mapping Out the Journey Ahead

Chase the vision, not the money; the money will end up following you.

-Tony Hsieh's

T HE FUNDAMENTAL TRUTH YOU must understand is that entrepreneurship is not just about profits—it's about purpose. I encourage you to enter the gateway of entrepreneurial exploration. Together, we embark on a journey to uncover the essence of venturing into the unknown. Dreams fuel this journey and determination drives it.

In this chapter, we inspect the heart of entrepreneurship, revealing its mysteries. We'll navigate the maze of definitions, showcasing the multifaceted parts of entrepreneurship. We'll explore its significance in today's dynamic landscape, understanding how it shapes economies, empowers individuals, and catalyzes innovation.

Our quest doesn't end there. With knowledge as our weapon, we will confront the challenges that lie ahead, forging a path through uncertainty and adversity. From financial hurdles to market competition, I'll equip you with the tools and strategies to overcome obstacles and emerge victorious. We'll discover the gems of wisdom and the pearls of insight that lead to success. With each lesson learned and each setback overcome, I'll hone your skills and sharpen your mind, mastering the art of entrepreneurship.

Embark on a transformative journey of discovery that will reshape your perception of success and empower you to pursue your vision, knowing that money will follow. I invite you to the world of entrepreneurship, where dreams take flight and possibilities are around every corner.

Lessons From Teen Entrepreneurs

Success as an entrepreneur typically requires careful planning, strategic decisions, and persistent effort. However, there are occasions when success seems to unfold effortlessly, almost by serendipity. In the world of entrepreneurship, there are stories of ventures that skyrocket to success, seemingly overnight. These instances serve as reminders that, while preparation and hard work are crucial, external factors and fortunate circumstances can also play a significant role in entrepreneurial triumphs. As we explore these experiences of teenage entrepreneurs, we encounter a diverse range of narratives. Some teens meticulously plan their ventures, executing each step with precision, while others stumble upon success unexpectedly, perhaps through a fortuitous encounter or a stroke of luck. Additionally, there are instances where what starts as a simple idea evolves into a thriving business, catching even the founders by surprise.

One notable example of teenage entrepreneurship began as a casual side business. From humble beginnings, it has become a household name, impacting countless lives. By examining the experiences of these companies, we can better comprehend the unpredictable nature of entrepreneurship and the potential for remarkable success to arise from unconventional origins. With this in mind, we embark on a journey to discover 6 businesses founded by teenagers. Each story showcases the diverse paths to entrepreneurial achievement and the limitless potential of young innovators, providing valuable lessons and inspiration.

1. **Injective Protocol—Eric Chen, 19**: Eric Chen's journey into entrepreneurship began during his high school years when he first explored blockchain technology by mining Bitcoin. This initial fascination evolved into the creation of Injective Protocol, a layer-2 decentralized exchange (DEX), co-founded with Albert Chon. Their venture caught the attention of major investors, including Mark Cuban, leading to a substantial $10 million funding round in 2021. Eric's story showcases how a teenage passion for technology can blossom into a groundbreaking business venture with global impact.

2. **Facebook—Mark Zuckerberg, 19**: Mark Zuckerberg's tale of entrepreneurship is legendary. As a college student at Harvard, he launched Facebook from his dorm room, envisioning a platform for connecting students. What started as a campus social network rapidly expanded into a global phenomenon, revolutionizing communication and connectivity. Today, Facebook boasts billions of users

worldwide and continues to shape the digital landscape. Mark's story exemplifies how a simple idea, fueled by passion and determination, can transform into a cultural phenomenon.

3. **WordPress—Matt Mullenweg, 19**: Matt Mullenweg's entrepreneurial journey began when he encountered a roadblock in his blogging endeavors. Undeterred by setbacks, Matt teamed up with Mike Little to create WordPress, a blogging platform that would redefine online publishing. Their user-friendly interface and open-source approach propelled WordPress to become the backbone of millions of websites worldwide. Matt's story illustrates how innovation and perseverance can lead to the creation of indispensable tools that empower individuals and businesses alike.

4. **Da Bomb Bath Fizzers—Caroline and Isabel Bercaw, 15 and 16**: Caroline and Isabel Bercaw's entrepreneurial spirit ignited at a young age when they identified a gap in the market for bath products. Dissatisfied with traditional bath bombs, they set out to create their own, infusing them with surprises and excitement. Their handmade creations gained traction at local fairs and soon caught the attention of retailers like Target. Today, Da Bomb Bath Fizzers is a thriving business, employing over a hundred people and delighting customers worldwide with their

innovative products. Caroline and Isabel's story exemplifies how youthful creativity and ingenuity can lead to entrepreneurial success.

5. **Dell—Michael Dell, 19**: Michael Dell's entrepreneurial journey began in his dorm room at the University of Texas, where he founded PC's Limited, later renamed Dell Computer Corporation. Michael's vision for customizable, affordable computers disrupted the industry and propelled Dell to become a global leader in technology. His story underscores the transformative power of innovative thinking and relentless execution, inspiring entrepreneurs to challenge the status quo and pursue their visions fearlessly.

6. **MinorMynas—Hillary Yip, 12**: Hillary Yip's entrepreneurial journey started with a personal challenge: learning a new language. Drawing from her experience, Hillary conceived MinorMynas, a video-sharing platform for language learners. Despite her young age, Hillary's determination and creativity propelled her to pitch her idea in entrepreneurship competitions, earning her recognition and support. Today, MinorMynas is empowering kids and teens worldwide to learn and connect through language, showcasing the potential of young entrepreneurs to drive meaningful change in their communities. Hillary's story is a testament to the bound-

less potential of youth-driven innovation and entre-preneurship.

Entrepreneurship for Teens 101

What is entrepreneurship?

Entrepreneurship is about seizing opportunities, taking cal-culated risks, and using your skills to create valuable business-es. For teens, it's about harnessing their fresh perspective to identify and actualize these opportunities.

Teens can take on entrepreneurship, too:

Contrary to popular belief, teens possess unique qualities that make them excellent entrepreneurs:

Fresh perspective: Teenagers bring new insights and innov-ative solutions to existing problems.

Bursting with energy: The youthful enthusiasm of teens fuels their drive to build and grow businesses.

Broad network: Teens have access to a diverse network of peers, mentors, and community members, providing valu-able feedback and support.

Tuned in: With a keen understanding of the latest trends and technology, teens are positioned to capitalize on emerging opportunities.

Willingness to take risks: Adolescence is a time for dreaming big and embracing calculated risks, with ample time to learn and pivot if necessary.

Benefits of entrepreneurship for teens:

Taking on the entrepreneurial journey offers numerous rewards, including:

- **Personal growth**: Holding multiple identities as an entrepreneur fosters skill development and self-discovery, enhancing one's personal and professional life.

- **Financial growth**: Successful ventures can lead to financial independence and provide valuable lessons in money management and financial literacy.

- **Independence and empowerment**: Entrepreneurship empowers teens to leverage their skills and resources to create income and pursue their passions, fostering confidence and self-reliance.

How to get started as a teenage entrepreneur:

Starting a business as a teen may seem daunting, but breaking it down into manageable steps can pave the way for success:

- **Identify your opportunity**: Explore your interests and passions to discover potential business ideas that add value to others.

- **Do market research**: Validate your idea by assessing market demand and identifying your target audience's needs.

- **Start small and build**: Begin with a minimally viable product or service, test it with customers, and iterate based on feedback.

- **Set clear goals**: Define your objectives and create a roadmap for achieving them, keeping yourself accountable along the way.

- **Get the word out**: Utilize your existing networks and explore marketing channels to promote your business and attract customers.

- **Get help**: Seek guidance from mentors, join entrepreneurship programs, and leverage resources to enhance your entrepreneurial journey.

Bring your dream business to life:

With determination, creativity, and access to resources, teens can transform their business ideas into reality, creating opportunities for themselves and positively impacting their communities. Embrace the journey of entrepreneurship, and who knows? Your venture might just change the world.

Vital Skills Every Teen Entrepreneur Needs

The journey of entrepreneurship requires a unique set of qualities and attributes. Here are some essential traits that aspiring teen entrepreneurs should focus on developing to increase their chances of success:

Strong leadership qualities: Successful entrepreneurs possess innate leadership abilities. They lead by example, communicate effectively, and inspire others to work towards a common goal. Developing leadership skills involves cultivating confidence, fostering teamwork, and earning the trust and respect of peers and collaborators.

Highly self-motivated: Success in business demands self-motivation and initiative. Teen entrepreneurs must be driven by a deep sense of purpose and passion for their endeavors. They should embrace challenges, remain resilient in the face of obstacles, and tirelessly pursue their goals with unwavering determination.

Strong sense of basic ethics and integrity: Upholding ethical standards is paramount. Teen entrepreneurs must demonstrate honesty, transparency, and integrity in all their dealings. Building a reputation for trustworthiness and reliability is essential for long-term business success.

Willingness to fail: Failure is an inevitable part of the entrepreneurial journey. Successful teen entrepreneurs embrace failure as an opportunity for growth and learning. They take calculated risks, learn from their mistakes, and persistently strive for improvement despite setbacks.

Serial innovators: Innovation lies at the heart of entrepreneurship. Teen entrepreneurs should cultivate a mindset of creativity, curiosity, and continuous improvement. They should constantly seek new ideas, challenge existing norms, and innovate solutions to address evolving needs and opportunities.

Know what you don't know: Effective teen entrepreneurs recognize the importance of humility and continuous learning. They are not afraid to seek guidance, ask questions, and leverage the expertise of others. By acknowledging their limitations and seeking knowledge, they can make informed decisions and navigate complex challenges more effectively.

Competitive spirit: Teen entrepreneurs thrive on competition and embrace challenges with enthusiasm. They are driven by a desire to excel, outperform competitors, and achieve success. Maintaining a competitive mindset fuels their ambition and their determination to succeed against all odds.

Understand the value of a strong peer network: Building a supportive network of peers, mentors, and collaborators is essential for teen entrepreneurs. They should actively cultivate relationships, seek mentorship, and leverage the expertise and resources of their network to overcome challenges and seize opportunities.

Focusing on developing these vital skills and qualities, aspiring teen entrepreneurs can enhance their capabilities and increase their chances of building successful and impactful businesses.

What It Means to Be a Teen Entrepreneur

Life as a teenage entrepreneur is a journey filled with excitement, challenges, and boundless growth opportunities. From my perspective, being a teen entrepreneur means embracing your entrepreneurial spirit and taking the initiative to turn your passions and hobbies into thriving businesses. For many teens, the journey begins with a spark of inspiration and a hobby they enjoy. Whether starting a blog, creating content, or exploring a new niche, the initial steps into entrepreneurship often feel like dipping your toes into uncharted waters. Currently, my husband and I run a publishing company and manage an eBay business. Recently, I also ventured into affiliate marketing.

In the past, I've explored various entrepreneurial endeavors. I once operated a handmade candle business, primarily selling through fundraisers for schools, clubs, and sports teams. Additionally, I experienced the handmade soap business. My journey into entrepreneurship took an unconventional route. After years in sales and management at a publishing company, I made a career shift to become a registered nurse at the age of 41. The decision stemmed from a deep-seated desire to make a meaningful difference in people's lives, which nursing fulfilled. During the COVID-19 pandemic, I served as a COVID nurse, but the toll of burnout and the limitations of hospital employment led me to pursue opportunities as a travel nurse. While financially lucrative, the constant travel made it challenging to sustain my handmade goods business-es. Eventually, I transitioned back to local nursing and found my way into publishing and affiliate marketing.

Entrepreneurship runs in my family's blood. My mother al-ways had a side business, initially crafting and selling dolls during Christmas to supplement income after my parents' di-vorce. Later, she ventured into photography, offering photo-copying and editing services. Similarly, my father, a mechanic, engaged in some side work to supplement our family income. Their example taught me the value of hard work and the versatility of alternative income streams beyond traditional employment.

From a young age, I exhibited an entrepreneurial spirit. In elementary school, I pretended to create my own brand of greeting cards- MissMark. I drew a logo and placed it on the back of handmade cards for my mom. Coincidentally, my first side hustle was selling greeting cards. During the summers, I earned fun products by selling Christmas cards in my neighborhood. In junior high babysitting became another avenue for earning money until I was old enough for formal employment.

The emergence of eBay reignited my entrepreneurial drive. While operating a daycare, I found equal—if not more—financial success selling collectibles on eBay. This experience solidified my desire to work for myself. Entrepreneurship has always been my calling, giving me a strong desire to avoid traditional employment. The allure of freedom and independence inherent in entrepreneurship has been my driving force.

One of the defining aspects of being a teenage entrepreneur is the freedom to explore and experiment with your ideas. Traditional jobs can feel constraining with rigid structures and expectations. Entrepreneurship is an opportunity to chart your course and pursue your interests with passion and determination. Of course, navigating the world of entrepreneurship as a teenager comes with unique challenges. Balancing schoolwork, extracurricular activities, and entrepreneurial pursuits requires careful time management and prioritization. However, these challenges also provide valuable lessons in resilience, resourcefulness, and adaptability that will serve you well in the long run.

One of the most rewarding aspects of being a teenage entrepreneur is the support and inspiration you might receive from your community. Whether from family, friends, or mentors, having a strong support network can make all the difference in your budding business. I've been fortunate to have supportive parents who encouraged my entrepreneurial endeavors while allowing me to maintain control and independence.

As you navigate the roadblocks and setbacks that inevitably arise, you'll learn to embrace failure as an opportunity for growth and self-improvement. Whether it's falling short of your goals or facing unexpected challenges, each setback teaches you valuable lessons and strengthens your understanding of how to succeed.

Despite the demands of entrepreneurship, it's essential to maintain a balance between your entrepreneurial pursuits and your personal life as a teenager. Engaging in extracurricular activities, spending time with friends, and pursuing your hobbies help you stay grounded and maintain a sense of normalcy amidst the demands of entrepreneurship.

Ultimately, being a teenage entrepreneur means having the courage to pursue your passions, the resilience to overcome challenges, and the determination to create a meaningful impact in the world. By embracing the entrepreneurial spirit within yourself and surrounding yourself with positivity and support, you can turn your dreams into reality and make a difference in your communities and beyond.

Advice for Teen Entrepreneurs

Choosing entrepreneurship as a teen can be both thrilling and daunting. However, with the right strategies and mindset, you can pave the way for success in the future. Here are some essential tips to help you kickstart your endeavors:

Take it one step at a time:

Building a business is a gradual process. Don't feel overwhelmed by trying to do everything at once. Focus on taking small, actionable steps towards your goals.

Lack of funds shouldn't be an excuse:

While having ample financial resources can be beneficial, it's not always necessary for starting a business. Many successful entrepreneurs began with minimal funds and built their ventures through creativity and determination.

Be committed:

Entrepreneurship requires dedication and perseverance. Stay committed to your goals, even when faced with challenges or setbacks.

Find your passion:

Building a business around something you're passionate about fuels your motivation and drive. Identify your interests and explore how to turn them into viable business ideas.

Get started and don't give up:

The hardest part of entrepreneurship is often getting started. Don't let fear or uncertainty hold you back. Take the first step towards your goals and keep pushing forward, even when things get tough.

Stay focused on your dream:

Keep your vision clear and stay focused on your long-term goals. Avoid getting distracted by short-term obstacles or setbacks.

Don't forget to network:

Building a strong network of mentors, peers, and industry professionals can provide valuable support and guidance. Don't hesitate to reach out to others for advice or assistance.

Prepare to make sacrifices:

Entrepreneurship requires dedication and sacrifice. Be prepared to invest time, effort, and resources into your business, even if it means making some personal sacrifices along the way.

Get your finances in order:

While you may not need significant funds to start a business, managing your finances wisely is essential. Start by building good credit and developing a solid financial plan for your venture.

Take action:

Planning is crucial, but taking action is what will ultimately drive your success. Be proactive and take decisive steps towards building and growing your business.

By staying focused on your goals, you can lay a strong foundation for your entrepreneurial journey and increase your chances of success. Remember it is an experience filled with learning opportunities and growth, so embrace the challenges and keep pushing forward towards your dreams.

Challenges and How to Overcome Them

Entrepreneurial ventures offer exciting prospects for young individuals but also come with their fair share of challenges. While these challenges may seem daunting, it's important to view them as opportunities for growth and learning. This section aims to shed light on the obstacles teen entrepreneurs may encounter and provide solutions to overcome them:

Staff recruitment:

Many young entrepreneurs often lack prior experience in managing personnel. When it comes to hiring their initial workforce, your managerial abilities are put to the test. Business ownership brings added pressure, especially when profitability is on the line. Establishing rules concerning working hours, vacation time, overtime compensation, and productivity becomes imperative.

Additionally, handling salary negotiations, addressing employee grievances, and, if necessary, terminating or laying off staff members are crucial responsibilities. Moreover, ensuring new hires possess the requisite skills and align with the company culture can mitigate challenges. Taking ample time to evaluate each candidate, conducting thorough reference checks, and remaining vigilant against superficial charm are essential steps in this process.

Navigating decision-making:

Transitioning from an employee to a business owner entails a significant shift in responsibility, particularly in decision-making. Every day, entrepreneurs are faced with myriad choices, ranging from minor details to pivotal judgments that could shape the future trajectory of their company. Among these decisions, those involving innovation and strategic direction hold particular significance. Whether it's revamping an underperforming aspect of the business or exploring new avenues for growth, entrepreneurs must possess the confidence to make bold decisions. While such responsibilities can induce stress and self-doubt, entrepreneurs must trust in their abilities and exercise sound judgment.

Building brand identity:

Establishing a strong brand image is paramount for young entrepreneurs. Building trust and credibility among customers is essential for the success of any business venture. Customers should perceive the entrepreneur as knowledgeable and proficient in their field of expertise. Prioritizing customer satisfaction and delivering high-quality products or services are integral to shaping a positive brand image. Actively addressing customer feedback and implementing necessary changes demonstrates a commitment to meeting customer needs. Ultimately, focusing on customer satisfaction rather than purely profit-driven motives fosters long-term success and sustainability in business endeavors.

Limited access to funding:

Securing capital is often a significant hurdle for young entrepreneurs. Unlike their older counterparts, who may have accumulated savings or access to investment networks, teens may struggle to finance their ventures. To address this, meticulous financial planning and seeking support from family, friends, or local financial institutions can provide essential funding.

Lack of experience:

Many teen entrepreneurs lack prior experience in managing people, making crucial business decisions, or navigating complex market dynamics. While this may pose challenges, you must embrace a learning mindset and seek guidance from mentors or educational resources to develop essential skills and knowledge.

Age stereotypes:

Young entrepreneurs may face skepticism or discrimination due to their age. Overcoming age-related biases requires you to demonstrate competence, professionalism, and determination in all business interactions. Building a strong personal brand and seeking supportive communities can help counteract negative stereotypes.

Market competition:

Competing in saturated markets or industries can be intimidating for young entrepreneurs. To stand out, it's crucial to focus on innovation, differentiation, and providing unique value to customers. Conducting thorough market research and identifying niche opportunities can give young entrepreneurs a competitive edge.

Balancing business and school:

Juggling academic commitments with entrepreneurial pursuits can be challenging. Effective time management, prioritization, and seeking support from mentors or peers can help teens strike a balance between their educational and business endeavors.

Navigating these challenges requires resilience, determination, and a willingness to learn from setbacks. By acknowledging and addressing these obstacles head-on, you pave the way for success and fulfillment in your entrepreneurial journey.

Mentorship and Networking

Networking is the practice of establishing a circle of individuals who can aid in accomplishing your objectives. Particularly crucial in the early stages of business development, networking holds significant importance for young entrepreneurs. It serves to interact with fellow business proprietors, providing avenues for guidance and encouragement. Networking facilitates opportunities for collaborations and partnerships, expediting business growth beyond solitary efforts. Furthermore, networking may lead to acquiring new clientele, a pivotal aspect for startups and small business proprietors. While constrained financial resources might limit advertising or extensive marketing endeavors, networking enables direct engagement with potential customers seeking the services or products offered by the company.

Crafting a distinctive personal brand is essential for young entrepreneurs, as it enhances credibility and showcases expertise effectively. This branding strategy aids in distinguishing oneself amidst competition and capturing the attention of prospective customers, collaborators, and investors.

To build connections effectively, entrepreneurs can employ various strategies, including leveraging online platforms, engaging with like-minded individuals, and participating in industry-related gatherings. Utilizing digital platforms allows for broadening networks beyond geographical boundaries while connecting with individuals sharing similar interests. This fosters meaningful relationships conducive to professional growth. Additionally, attending industry events provides opportunities for face-to-face interactions, facilitating deeper connections and potential collaborations.

Finding networking opportunities can be accomplished through diligent research on industry-related events, active participation in business organizations, and direct outreach via social media platforms or email. Entrepreneurial boot camps and similar programs offer additional avenues for networking, and facilitating interactions with industry mentors and fellow teenage entrepreneurs, thereby expanding collaboration prospects.

Recognizing the significance of networking in the entrepreneurial journey is pivotal for young business owners. Establishing connections with potential clients, investors, and mentors lays the groundwork for business growth and personal development. Embracing authenticity, approachability, and helpfulness in networking endeavors fosters genuine connections. This paves the way for mutually beneficial relationships and sustained success.

What a Mentor Does

Navigating entrepreneurship as a young adult can be daunting, with the juggling act of classes, work, extracurricular commitments, and personal obligations. However, having a mentor can significantly alleviate these challenges. By investing a bit of time and effort, it's feasible to establish a network of mentors who can profoundly impact your entrepreneurial journey.

While the frequency of interactions may vary—ranging from weekly discussions to sporadic meetings—each exchange holds immense value. Mentors, having traversed the path you're embarking on, offer a wealth of invaluable insights, guidance, moral support, and encouragement essential for your success. From imparting wisdom on time and financial management to aiding in the attainment of personal and professional objectives, mentors serve as trusted advisors and confidants. A proficient mentor adeptly navigates you through common entrepreneurial hurdles such as securing funding, managing growth, resolving partnership conflicts, and grappling with ethical dilemmas.

The Importance of Mentorship for Young Entrepreneurs

Mentorship serves as a transformative relationship crucial for the growth of young entrepreneurs, providing invaluable knowledge, support, and perspective essential for their business journey.

Why is mentorship important?

Networking Opportunities: Mentors boast extensive networks, facilitating introductions to industry professionals, investors, and potential partners, thereby expanding the horizons of young entrepreneurs:

Skill development: Through personalized guidance and resources, mentors assist in identifying and honing the required skills and competencies crucial for success.

Objective feedback: Mentors offer constructive criticism, aiding in refining ideas, strategies, and decision-making processes.

Emotional support: Mentorship provides a vital pillar of emotional support, offering encouragement and motivation to navigate the highs and lows of the business world.

Expanded perspectives: Mentors provide alternative viewpoints, encouraging young entrepreneurs to think creatively and explore new avenues.

Accountability and goal setting: Mentors foster accountability and help set achievable goals, ensuring progress and momentum in the entrepreneurial journey.

Confidence building: By instilling belief in the mentee's potential, mentors bolster confidence and empower young entrepreneurs to take calculated risks.

Personal growth: Mentorship nurtures self-awareness, resilience, and essential leadership qualities, fostering personal development.

Long-term guidance: Mentors serve as trusted advisors, offering ongoing support beyond the initial mentorship period, and guiding young entrepreneurs throughout their journey.

Tailoring mentorship for success

- **Finding the right mentor**: Seek mentors with relevant industry experience and compatible values, ensuring a fruitful and impactful mentorship relationship.

- **Setting clear goals and expectations**: Define specific objectives and expectations for the mentorship, aligning them with personal and professional aspirations.

- **Regular communication and feedback**: Maintain open lines of communication with mentors. Schedule regular check-ins and solicit feedback to optimize learning and growth.

Common Mistakes by Teen Entrepreneurs

Teen entrepreneurs often exhibit remarkable creativity and ambition in launching their businesses, yet many fall prey to avoidable pitfalls that can jeopardize their ventures. Here are some prevalent mistakes and strategies to steer clear of them:

Neglecting costs:

Many young entrepreneurs overlook the true costs of running their businesses, failing to factor in expenses beyond the obvious. For instance, expenses like transportation, meals, and equipment maintenance can significantly impact profitability and should be accounted for in pricing strategies.

Counting sales as profit:

It's a common misconception among teen entrepreneurs to equate sales revenue with profit. However, true profit is determined by subtracting all expenses, including borrowed funds, from revenue. Failing to distinguish between revenue and profit can lead to financial mismanagement and debt accumulation.

Sales assumptions:

Relying solely on family and friends as customers can create a false sense of success. While initial support from loved ones is valuable, sustainable businesses must appeal to a broader market. Teen entrepreneurs should conduct market research to validate their assumptions and identify potential customers beyond their immediate circles.

Lack of planning:

Optimism is admirable, but it must be complemented by realistic planning and execution. Successful businesses require meticulous planning and efficient operations. Teen entrepreneurs should invest time in developing comprehensive business plans and anticipate challenges to avoid setbacks.

Poor time management:

Balancing school, extracurricular activities and business endeavors demands effective time management. Teen entrepreneurs must prioritize tasks, set achievable goals, and allocate time wisely to avoid burnout and ensure productivity.

Being too impatient:

Impatience can lead to hasty decisions and premature expansion efforts. Teen entrepreneurs should resist the urge to rush growth and focus on building a solid foundation for their businesses. Patience, perseverance, and strategic growth plans are keys to long-term success.

Trying to do everything alone:

Many teen entrepreneurs attempt to handle every aspect of their businesses independently, leading to overwhelm and inefficiency. It's essential to delegate tasks, seek assistance from mentors or advisors, and build a reliable support network to foster growth and alleviate stress.

Hiring the wrong people:

Inadequate hiring practices can undermine business operations and culture. Teen entrepreneurs should prioritize hiring individuals who align with their vision, values, and work ethic. Thorough screening, interviewing, and onboarding processes can help identify suitable candidates and mitigate hiring mistakes.

Not understanding your market:

Lack of market awareness can result in misguided product development and ineffective marketing strategies. Teen entrepreneurs should conduct market research to understand consumer needs, preferences, and behaviors. Regular feedback and adaptation are essential for staying relevant and competitive in the market.

Summary

Now that we've explored the fundamentals of entrepreneurship and the challenges that come with it, we're ready to go deeper into the qualities and approaches that set successful entrepreneurs apart. In the next chapter, we'll jump into the mindset and skills required to thrive in the entrepreneurial world, providing you with the tools and insights needed to cultivate a winning mindset and navigate your own path to success.

Chapter 2

Think Like an Entrepreneur

*Being an entrepreneur is a mindset. You have to
see things as opportunities all the time. I like to do
interviews. I like to push people on certain topics. I
like to dig into the stories where there's not neces-
sarily a right or wrong answer.*

–Joseph Pilates

E NTREPRENEURSHIP IS MORE THAN just starting a business; it's a way of thinking and approaching the world.
In this chapter, we explore the essential qualities and approaches that define successful entrepreneurs. Drawing inspiration from the words above, we can comprehend how
adopting the teen entrepreneurial mindset can lead to identifying opportunities in every situation.

Throughout this chapter, you will discover the importance
of seeing challenges as opportunities for growth, embracing
curiosity and tenacity, and cultivating resilience in the face
of adversity. I'll provide practical strategies for developing a
young entrepreneurial mindset, from fostering creativity and
innovation to maintaining a positive attitude amid uncertainty. Whether you're a seasoned entrepreneur or just starting your journey, this chapter guides you to cultivate the right
mindset for success. By harnessing the power of entrepreneurial thinking, you'll be better equipped to navigate the
challenges and seize the opportunities that come your way.

Understanding the Entrepreneurial Mindset

Can an entrepreneurial mindset be taught? The evidence suggests that yes, it can. Entrepreneurship education, particularly when introduced at a young age, has been shown to develop specific skills crucial for success in business and beyond. This mindset, often described as a set of tools for life, equips individuals with the resilience, creativity, and problem-solving abilities necessary for navigating the challenges of the modern world. The Network for Teaching Entrepreneurship (NFTE) has developed a framework for defining the entrepreneurial mindset, drawing on years of experience teaching entrepreneurship to young people. This framework identifies eight core domains that characterize entrepreneurial thinking, encompassing characteristics, attitudes, behaviors, and skills essential for seizing opportunities, overcoming setbacks, and achieving success in diverse settings.

8 Domains of Critical Entrepreneurial Thinking

But can this mindset be measured? NFTE has taken on the challenge of developing and measuring the entrepreneurial mindset through the Entrepreneurial Mindset Index (EMI). Collaborating with researchers from the Educational Testing Service (ETS) and with support from EY, NFTE designed the EMI to assess mastery across the eight core domains identified as critical to entrepreneurial thinking. This tool serves as a reliable instrument for measuring entrepreneurial mindset, providing students with valuable insights into their strengths and areas for growth. What exactly is the Entrepreneurial Mindset Index (EMI)? It's more than just an assessment tool; it's a resource for students and educators alike. By completing the EMI, students receive personalized reports detailing their entrepreneurial mindsets, including their top three self-reported domains. These reports help students identify their entrepreneurial archetype, guiding them as they embark on their entrepreneurial journey. Moreover, students can track their progress and growth throughout NFTE programs.

But why is an entrepreneurial mindset important? In today's rapidly evolving economy, success is not solely determined by traditional cognitive skills; noncognitive skills, such as critical thinking and problem-solving, are equally crucial. The entrepreneurial mindset combines these foundational skills with entrepreneurial abilities demanded by the innovation economy, making it indispensable for engaging in school, enhancing educational performance, and gaining favor with employers. Ultimately, teaching the entrepreneurial mindset isn't just about preparing students for entrepreneurship; it's about empowering them for success in higher education, the military, and all aspects of life. By instilling the entrepreneurial mindset, NFTE programs bridge educational gaps, foster inclusivity, and accelerate gender diversity in entrepreneurship, paving the way for a future workforce armed with the skills needed for high-wage jobs and lifelong success.

Employee vs. Entrepreneurial Mindset

Understanding the difference between an employee mindset and an entrepreneurial mindset is crucial for anyone considering venturing into the business world. While both paths have their merits, recognizing the distinctions can illuminate why an entrepreneurial mindset often holds the edge:

Security vs. freedom: Employees often seek the security of a stable job, valuing regular paychecks, benefits, and clearly defined tasks. In contrast, entrepreneurs embrace the uncertainty of freedom, foregoing regular paychecks and benefits to pursue their vision. This freedom requires adept self-management to maximize its potential.

Held accountable vs. self-accountable: Employees answer to a boss, while entrepreneurs are their own bosses, requiring a high degree of self-discipline. Transitioning from being told what to do to self-accountability can be challenging but is essential for entrepreneurial success.

Saying yes vs. saying no: Employees may prioritize saying yes to please their superiors, while entrepreneurs master the art of saying no to focus on high-return opportunities. Effective prioritization is key to optimizing resources and efforts.

DIY vs. delegate: Employees often take on tasks themselves to impress their bosses, while entrepreneurs leverage delegation to maximize efficiency. Recognizing the value of time management and delegation is vital for entrepreneurial effectiveness.

Safety vs. risk: Employees value safety and stability, whereas entrepreneurs are willing to embrace risk and uncertainty as part of their journey. Embracing risk requires a mindset shift from seeking safety to pursuing growth and innovation.

Balance vs. seasons: Employees strive for work-life balance, seeking equal attention in all areas of life. Entrepreneurs recognize that balance is elusive and instead focus on seasons, prioritizing different areas of life at different times.

Fixed vs. flexible time management: Employees excel at meeting deadlines within a fixed schedule, while entrepreneurs must adapt to flexible time management due to the diverse demands of their roles.

Now vs. future mindset: Employees focus on daily tasks, while entrepreneurs keep their eyes on the future, aligning current actions with long-term goals and vision.

Technician vs. driver: Employees are specialists in their roles, focusing solely on their assigned tasks, while entrepreneurs drive the vision of their business, assuming various roles and responsibilities to steer toward success.

An Entrepreneurial Mindset = Lifelong Growth

Embracing an entrepreneurial mindset offers numerous benefits beyond just succeeding in a competitive environment. Here are some additional advantages of nurturing this mindset:

Execution over ideas:

While ideas are abundant, the ability to execute them effectively is what sets successful entrepreneurs apart. This skill of turning ideas into tangible outcomes is valuable not only in business but in all aspects of life.

Adaptability to change:

Entrepreneurship is akin to building a plane while flying it, as once aptly described. Adapting to constant changes, feedback, and evolving customer needs requires an entrepreneurial mindset that thrives on innovation and flexibility.

Key to sustainability:

In a world marked by shifting economies and constant disruption, an entrepreneurial mindset is key to sustainability. It enables individuals to navigate uncertainties, identify emerging opportunities, and pivot strategies accordingly, ensuring long-term viability and success.

Embracing failure as learning:

Developing an entrepreneurial mindset involves embracing failure as a natural part of the journey. Instead of seeing setbacks as roadblocks, entrepreneurs view them as valuable learning opportunities that propel growth and innovation.

Cultivating growth muscles:

The entrepreneurial mindset involves continuous learning and growth, not just in business but also in personal development. Engaging in diverse experiences, challenging oneself, and seeking opportunities to stretch beyond comfort zones are all ways to strengthen these "growth muscles."

Switching to an abundant mindset:

Shifting from a mindset of scarcity to one of abundance is crucial for entrepreneurs. An abundance mindset fosters openness to new opportunities, creativity in problem-solving, and the ability to create opportunities by connecting dots and applying learned knowledge.

How to Think Like an Entrepreneur

To develop an entrepreneurial mindset, it's crucial to embody key attributes and characteristics that define this approach to life and work:

Embrace creativity: Entrepreneurs thrive on innovation and creativity, constantly seeking new ways to solve problems and improve existing processes.

Learn from failure: Rather than viewing failure as a setback, entrepreneurs see it as an opportunity for growth and learning. They analyze their mistakes, extract valuable lessons, and use them to refine their approach.

Take calculated risks: Entrepreneurial success often requires stepping out of comfort zones and taking risks. However, these risks are not impulsive; instead, they are calculated and based on thorough analysis and assessment.

Develop a growth mindset: Entrepreneurs possess a mindset geared towards continuous learning and improvement. They believe abilities and intelligence can be developed through dedication and hard work.

Persist and stay resilient: In the face of challenges and setbacks, entrepreneurs display resilience and perseverance. They remain determined to overcome obstacles and achieve their goals, even during adversity.

Think strategically: Entrepreneurs have a knack for thinking strategically, envisioning the bigger picture, and planning for long-term success. They assess situations holistically and make decisions that align with their overarching objectives.

Foster effective communication: Clear and effective communication is essential for entrepreneurs to convey their vision, build relationships, and inspire others. They excel at articulating ideas, listening actively, and collaborating with diverse stakeholders.

Cultivate a problem-solving attitude: Entrepreneurs approach problems as opportunities for innovation and growth. They are resourceful, adaptable, and adept at finding creative solutions to complex challenges.

Nurturing Your Inner Entrepreneur

To nurture and develop an entrepreneurial mindset, consider these tips:

Commit to your passion: Starting a business can be challenging, so it's crucial to have a strong passion for what you're doing. Your passion will drive you through the inevitable obstacles and setbacks.

Understand market needs: Before taking on entrepreneurship, thoroughly research and understand the needs of your target market. This understanding will help you tailor your products or services to meet those needs effectively.

Plan your vision and build a strategy: Create a clear vision for your entrepreneurial venture and develop a strategic plan to achieve it. Having a roadmap will guide your actions and keep you focused on your goals.

Network with other entrepreneurs: Surround yourself with like-minded individuals who can offer support, advice, and inspiration. Networking with other entrepreneurs can provide valuable insights and opportunities for collaboration.

Learn from your setbacks: Failure is an inevitable part of entrepreneurship, but it's how you respond to setbacks that matter. Embrace failure as a learning opportunity, analyze what went wrong, and use those lessons to strengthen your entrepreneurial mindset.

By committing to your passion, understanding market needs, planning strategically, networking with peers, and learning from setbacks, you can develop and nurture a resilient and innovative entrepreneurial mindset.

Entrepreneurial Thinking in Action

To follow are 7 real-world examples that illustrate how entrepreneurial thinking can lead to innovative solutions, resilience in the face of challenges, and a positive impact on communities:

1. **Resourcefulness**: During a winter storm in Texas, fast food restaurants used hamburger buns to insulate their pipes, demonstrating resourcefulness in finding innovative solutions with available materials.

2. **Problem-Solving:** A six-year-old named Eisha noticed a lack of colorful and fun mask options for kids during the pandemic. She created unique designs and sold them in vending machines, showcasing problem-solving skills and creativity.

3. **Opportunity Seeking**: When Reece's dog developed allergies to most treats, Reece saw an opportunity instead of a setback. He created a business providing allergen-free treats, demonstrating an eye for spotting opportunities in challenges.

4. **Empathy**: During a crisis, the H-E-B supermarket chain in Texas not only provided food and water but also kindness and comfort to their customers, showing empathy and understanding of their needs.

5. **Persistence & Grit**: A 17-year-old entrepreneur named Victoria faced challenges while bringing her idea of combining charm bracelets and glasses to life. Despite setbacks, she persisted and turned her idea into a successful business, highlighting the importance of persistence and grit.

6. **Embracing Failure**: A card company initially failed its attempts to provide protective gear during the pandemic. Instead of giving up, they learned from their mistakes and improved their designs, demonstrating resilience and a willingness to learn from failure.

7. **Optimism**: Despite the challenges of online schooling due to COVID-19, a six-year-old girl named Zoe found ways to bring joy and togetherness to her community, showcasing optimism and a positive outlook in the face of adversity.

Summary

As we conclude this chapter on cultivating an entrepreneurial mindset, it's essential to reflect on the key qualities and approaches that define successful entrepreneurs. Throughout this journey, we've explored the importance of determination, problem-solving, empathy, and resilience in navigating the challenges of entrepreneurship. Embrace these qualities and adopt the right mindset, to lay a strong foundation for your entrepreneurial journey.

Looking ahead, the next chapter will go deep into a critical aspect of entrepreneurship: identifying your passions and interests. I'll provide the tools and insights to uncover what truly excites and motivates you. Understanding your passions is crucial for aligning your personal and professional pursuits, ultimately leading to increased satisfaction, motivation, and growth opportunities. Moreover, we'll explore business ideas that require little to no capital, offering practical strategies for aspiring entrepreneurs to kickstart their ventures.

Get ready to discover your passions, explore new opportunities, and embark on an exciting journey towards entrepreneurial success.

Chapter 3

Finding Your Path Through Passion

*The only way to do great work is to love what you
do. If you haven't found it yet, keep looking. Don't
settle.*

                                                    –Steve Jobs

T HE WORDS ABOVE RESONATE deeply with anyone
     searching for fulfillment and success. In this chapter,
we take on the journey to uncover the essence of these words,
jumping into the realm of passions and interests. Passion is
the fuel that drives extraordinary accomplishments, the spark
that ignites innovation, and the compass that guides us toward meaningful endeavors. Yet, identifying our passions and
interests can sometimes feel like searching for a needle in a
haystack. But fear not, for this chapter provides you with
the tools and insights necessary to embark on this journey of
self-discovery.

By the end of this chapter, you will understand the significance of aligning your passions with your pursuits and be
equipped with practical strategies to unearth your true calling. We'll explore various methods and exercises to help you
uncover what truly excites and motivates you, paving the way
for a more fulfilling and purpose-driven life. Moreover, we'll
explore the sphere of entrepreneurship, unveiling business
ideas that require minimal capital investment. Whether you
dream of starting a venture of your own or simply seek to

infuse more passion into your current endeavors, this chapter empowers you to take the first step towards a future filled with excitement, satisfaction, and boundless possibilities for growth. So, let's embark on this journey of self-discovery and unlock the door to a world where passion meets purpose.

Career vs. Entrepreneurship Choosing the Right Path

Deciding on a career path is a pivotal moment in life, shaping our trajectory and influencing our overall well-being. Yet, amidst the multitude of options, one crucial decision often goes overlooked: the choice between a traditional career and the path of entrepreneurship. In essence, the disparity between these two paths lies in the fundamental principles of career (employment) versus self-employment.

Career

While a traditional career offers stability, defined roles, and predetermined earnings within the confines of an organization, entrepreneurship embodies autonomy, risk-taking, and the pursuit of one's vision. As employees, individuals trade autonomy for security, committing to fulfill specific duties outlined by an employer in exchange for a steady income and benefits.

Entrepreneurship

Conversely, entrepreneurs embrace the uncertainty of self-employment, assuming full responsibility for their organization's success or failure while enjoying the freedom to dictate their workload, schedule, and strategic direction. Yet, entrepreneurship is not for the faint of heart. It demands resilience, perseverance, and a willingness to navigate through uncertainty. While the journey may be arduous, the rewards can be profound, offering unparalleled fulfillment and the opportunity to sculpt one's destiny.

How do you know if entrepreneurship is right for you?

It requires a deep introspection of your aspirations, values, and risk tolerance. If you possess an insatiable drive to challenge the status quo, a hunger for autonomy, and a thirst for innovation, then entrepreneurship may be your calling. However, taking on the entrepreneurial journey necessitates thorough preparation and a willingness to embrace lifelong learning. Seek mentorship, cultivate a strong educational foundation, and immerse yourself in networking opportunities to fortify your entrepreneurial acumen and mitigate risks.

Ultimately, whether you choose the path of entrepreneurship or opt for a traditional career, the key lies in making an informed decision aligned with your personal aspirations and professional goals. So, dive into the depths of self-discovery, weigh the pros and cons, and choose a path that resonates most profoundly with your inner calling.

Why Passion Is Important

Defining entrepreneurial passion

Entrepreneurial passion is a cornerstone of entrepreneurial success, driving individuals to pursue their goals with unwavering enthusiasm and dedication. While its precise influence on entrepreneurial success has been a topic of debate in academic circles, recent research sheds light on its significance. Drawing upon the theory of social information processing, this research investigates the internal mechanisms through which entrepreneurial passion influences entrepreneurial success. It further examines how individual psychological capital, coupled with external entrepreneurial policy support, amplifies the impact of entrepreneurial passion on success.

Through extensive questionnaire surveys of entrepreneurs across various entrepreneurship hubs, the findings reveal a compelling connection between entrepreneurial passion, psychological capital, and success. Entrepreneurial passion emerges as a catalyst, bolstering individuals' psychological capital and fostering a positive trajectory toward success. Moreover, the study highlights the mediating role of psychological capital, elucidating how it bridges the gap between entrepreneurial passion and success. Additionally, the research underscores the instrumental role of entrepreneurship policy support in enhancing the effects of entrepreneurial passion by facilitating the accumulation of psychological capital.

Ultimately, these insights underscore the importance of cultivating entrepreneurial passion and leveraging external support mechanisms to optimize the path to entrepreneurial success. By understanding and harnessing the interplay between passion, psychological capital, and policy support, entrepreneurs can enhance their resilience, creativity, and ultimately, their chances of success in the entrepreneurial landscape.

Why is passion vital for entrepreneurship and crafting a flourishing business?

Entrepreneurship is a journey fueled by passion, a driving force that propels individuals toward their goals with unwavering determination and enthusiasm. Harnessing passion not only ignites the entrepreneurial spirit but also plays a pivotal role in shaping a thriving business. Here's why passion is essential for entrepreneurial success:

Motivation:

Passion infuses your endeavors with fervor and zeal, fueling your determination to overcome challenges and achieve your goals. When you're passionate about your work, each step forward becomes a stride toward your vision.

Conviction:

Passion imbues you with an unwavering belief in your mission, making you more convincing in your interactions with clients, partners, and stakeholders. Your genuine enthusiasm resonates with others, inspiring trust and confidence in your brand.

Resilience:

In the face of adversity, passion serves as a resilience anchor, enabling you to weather storms and persevere through obstacles. It fuels your resilience, empowering you to bounce back stronger from setbacks.

Enjoyment of the journey:

A passion-driven pursuit is inherently fulfilling, making the entrepreneurial journey a gratifying and enjoyable experience. Embracing your passions transforms challenges into opportunities for growth and self-discovery.

Clarity in uncertainty:

During moments of uncertainty or indecision, passion provides clarity, guiding your decisions and actions toward alignment with your core values and aspirations. It serves as a compass, navigating you through uncharted waters.

Establishment of core values:

Passionate entrepreneurship fosters the establishment of core values that define your business ethos and principles. These values serve as the bedrock of your organization, guiding its culture and decision-making processes.

Motivation and confidence:

With passion as your driving force, you are propelled by a sense of purpose and conviction in your mission. This intrinsic motivation instills confidence in your abilities, empowering you to pursue your entrepreneurial endeavors with unwavering determination.

Networking and collaboration:

Passion cultivates genuine connections with like-minded individuals who share your vision and values. It facilitates meaningful networking opportunities and collaborations, enriching your entrepreneurial journey with diverse perspectives and experiences.

Expertise and authority:

Immersed in your passion, you become an authority in your field, owning your space and contributing valuable insights and expertise. Passion fuels continuous learning and growth, enabling you to stay ahead of the curve and innovate within your industry.

Differentiation:

Passion sets you apart from competitors, infusing your brand with authenticity and sincerity. It resonates with your audience on a deeper level, fostering lasting connections and loyalty.

In essence, passion is the cornerstone of entrepreneurial success, guiding you toward fulfillment, purpose, and prosperity. As you embark on your entrepreneurial journey, embrace your passions wholeheartedly, and let them light the path to a thriving and impactful business. Remember, a passionate entrepreneur is destined for success and poised to make a meaningful difference in the world.

Successful Teen Entrepreneurs with Passion

Teenage entrepreneurs driven by passion are carving their paths in the business world, debunking the traditional notion that success only comes through conventional routes like education and employment. These young trailblazers are leveraging their talents and passions to create thriving ventures, propelled by the vast reach of social media platforms like Instagram, TikTok, and YouTube:

- Take Milly, for instance, a 15-year-old makeup enthusiast who turned her passion for beauty into a flourishing online presence. By sharing makeup tutorials and skincare tips on Instagram and YouTube, Milly not only showcases her skills but also engages with her audience, fostering a sense of connection and community. Her advice to aspiring entrepreneurs? Just go for it, push yourself, and most importantly, have fun along the way.

- Similarly, Mel, a 17-year-old writer and YouTuber, found success by self-publishing her debut novel and harnessing the power of social media to connect with fellow writers and readers. She emphasizes the importance of joining online communities to not only market your work but also build meaningful relationships and find support along the journey.

- Evan, a 15-year-old self-taught photographer, uses Instagram as a platform to showcase his stunning visual artistry and inspire others. His advice to budding photographers? Keep your options open and embrace every opportunity that comes your way.

- Ticha, although no longer a teenager, started her career early by winning a reality TV competition and leveraging social media to build her brand as a model and influencer. Her relentless pursuit of perfection and dedication to her craft serve as inspiration for aspiring entrepreneurs.

- Lastly, Catherine, a 17-year-old photographer, stumbled upon her passion for photography and transformed it into a thriving business through Instagram. Her advice to fellow photographers? Be unique, and let your passion drive you towards your dreams.

These stories illustrate the transformative power of passion in entrepreneurship. When fueled by genuine enthusiasm and dedication, passion inspires creativity, resilience, and innovation. It empowers young entrepreneurs to overcome challenges, seize opportunities, and create impactful ventures that resonate with their audience. With social media as a powerful marketing tool and a wealth of resources at their disposal, there has never been a better time for teens to embark on their entrepreneurial journeys. So, what are you waiting for? Embrace your passion, unleash your creativity, and start building the business of your dreams today.

Cultivating passion for your business

Passion is the driving force behind successful start-ups. Without it, navigating the challenges of entrepreneurship becomes significantly more arduous. So, how can you cultivate passion for your startup? Here are some strategies:

Embrace your product or service:

Passion begins with belief. If you're genuinely enthusiastic about the value your product or service offers, your passion will naturally follow suit. Take the time to understand the problem your offering solves and the impact it can have on people's lives. This belief will fuel your dedication and drive.

Align with a meaningful mission:

Being mission-driven adds depth to your passion. Define a clear mission for your startup that resonates with your values and goals. This overarching purpose will serve as a guiding light during challenging times, reinforcing your commitment to your venture's success.

Foster a stellar team:

Surround yourself with individuals who share your passion and vision. Building a great team not only enhances the collective drive but also creates a supportive environment where passion thrives. Collaborating with like-minded individuals who are equally passionate about the product or service cultivates a sense of camaraderie and inspires mutual motivation.

Cultivate persistence:

Persistence is the cornerstone of entrepreneurial success. There will inevitably be obstacles and setbacks along the journey, but passion fuels perseverance. When faced with adversity, tap into your passion for your start-up to find the resilience needed to push forward. Remember, every challenge presents an opportunity for growth and learning.

Debunking Passion Myths

Passion is often romanticized as the key to finding fulfillment and success in life. However, there are several myths surrounding the concept of passion that need to be debunked:

Myth: It's so hard to find your passion.

- **Reality**: While discovering your passion may require exploration and introspection, it's not an impossible task. Passion can evolve over time and may manifest in unexpected ways. Instead of waiting for a lightning bolt moment, focus on exploring your interests and engaging in activities that energize you.

Myth: You need to find your passion by a certain age, date, or point in your life.

- **Reality**: There's no deadline for finding your passion. It's a lifelong journey of self-discovery, and it's never too late to pursue what excites you. Your interests and priorities may evolve over time, so remain open to new opportunities and experiences at any stage of life.

Myth: You can't earn any money doing things that you're passionate about, and you should stay in a job you hate for the money.

- **Reality**: While it's true that not every passion will

lead to financial success, it's possible to monetize your interests with creativity and strategic planning. Pursuing work you're passionate about can lead to greater job satisfaction and fulfillment, ultimately enhancing your overall well-being.

Myth: It's not passion unless it's often.

- **Reality**: Passion doesn't have to be all-consuming or constant. It's normal for interests to fluctuate and evolve. Embrace the ebb and flow of passion, allowing yourself to explore different avenues and adapt to changing circumstances.

Myth: Passion is all it takes to create success or do what you love, and money will follow.

- **Reality**: While passion is important, it's not the sole predictor of success. Building a sustainable career or business requires strategic planning, hard work, and perseverance. Passion alone may not guarantee financial stability or achievement, so it's essential to pair passion with practical skills and a solid business strategy.

Identifying Your Entrepreneurial Passion

Discovering your entrepreneurial passion entails introspection and exploration. Here are some questions to guide you along the path:

What are your hobbies?

Your hobbies often reflect your passions. Whether it's gardening, sports, or art, your hobbies can provide valuable insights into your potential entrepreneurial pursuits.

What are your natural talents?

Your innate talents can serve as clues to your passions. Consider what comes naturally to you and explore how to leverage these talents in your entrepreneurial endeavors.

What activities bring you joy?

Joyful activities often indicate areas of passion. Pay attention to the tasks that make you feel fulfilled and satisfied—they could hold the key to your entrepreneurial passion.

What topics do you enjoy learning about?

Your curiosity and thirst for knowledge can point you toward your passions. Identify the subjects that captivate your interest and delve deeper into them to uncover potential business ideas.

What challenges do you naturally want to solve?

Your inclination toward solving certain problems can reveal your passions. Reflect on the issues or challenges that resonate with you and consider how you can address them through entrepreneurship.

What is your ultimate career goal?

Envision your ideal career path and consider what type of work would bring you fulfillment. Your dream job can offer valuable insights into your entrepreneurial passions.

Transforming Your Passion into Profit

When transforming your passion into a lucrative endeavor, the initial step involves pinpointing your specialized area. This requires introspection into your hobbies and interests to unearth where your true passions lie. Take a moment to contemplate activities that bring you fulfillment, regardless of what it may be. For instance, if you're enthusiastic about fitness and enjoy experimenting with various workout routines, you might explore opportunities within the health and wellness sector. Specializing in crafting compelling content to motivate others towards a healthy lifestyle could position you as a sought-after freelance fitness writer.

Once potential interests are identified, it's crucial to evaluate your skill set and expertise. Reflect on the competencies gained through formal education, work experience, or personal pursuits. Whether you possess a flair for graphic design, a talent for photography, or expertise in a specific domain, your skills can direct you toward profitable niches. For instance, if you're skilled in graphic design and enjoy creating visually striking content, focusing on providing design services for businesses in niche sectors like tech start-ups could be lucrative. By narrowing down to a specialty such as logo design and branding, you can establish yourself as an authority and attract clients who value your specialized talents.

While passion and proficiency are vital, assessing market demand and competition are equally important. Conduct research to identify niches where your skills are sought after and where you can distinguish yourself from competitors. Look for unexplored market areas or underserved segments that align with your passion and expertise. For instance, if you're passionate about sustainable living, niches like zero-waste products or eco-friendly home décor could be worth exploring. Conduct thorough market research to gauge demand and competition within each niche, aiding in informed decision-making about which niche to pursue.

Lastly, once a potential niche is identified, it's time to test your concepts and gather feedback. Begin by creating sample work or offering services on a small scale to gauge responses from your target audience. This could entail building a portfolio, launching a website, or soliciting feedback from potential clients. For instance, if you're considering venturing into pet photography, offering complimentary or discounted sessions to pet owners in your locale can help showcase your skills, expand your portfolio, and gather valuable insights from clients.

From Passion to Paycheck

Exploring Business Ideas

By following these steps, you can identify your passion and carve out your niche of freelance entrepreneurship. Remember, discovering a niche that aligns with your interests, skills, and market demand is pivotal to monetizing your passion. Crafting an ideal business idea as a teen involves considering your individual circumstances and aspirations. Here's a closer look at important factors.

Let's examine the essential components:

Passion and interest:

It's crucial to pursue business concepts that resonate with your passions and interests. When teens are genuinely enthusiastic about their endeavors, it sparks motivation and ingenuity. For example, a teenager passionate about gardening might discover fulfillment in establishing a vegetable supplier business, while a tech-savvy teen might explore possibilities in hardware and software development.

Low start-up costs:

Given the financial limitations often encountered by teenagers, it's vital to select business ideas that are financially viable to initiate. Ventures with minimal start-up expenses, such as refreshment stands, gaming stations, or selling candy, can help surmount financial obstacles. These endeavors typically necessitate only a small initial investment, making them attainable for teens.

Flexible schedule:

Teens lead busy lives, balancing academics, extracurricular activities, and social engagements. Thus, their business concept needs to offer flexibility regarding working hours. Part-time or freelance opportunities, such as social media management or tutoring, enable teens to adapt their work to accommodate their busy schedules.

Scalability:

While commencing with modest ventures is prudent, it's also crucial for the business concept to possess potential for expansion. Teens can explore scalable enterprises like e-commerce or app development, which can grow as their skills and resources develop.

By considering these factors, teenagers can embark on entrepreneurial endeavors that align with their interests and cater to their individual life circumstances.

Ideal Businesses for Teens

Initiating a business venture as a teenager without any up-front investment is plausible. Let's explore various business categories tailored to teens, encompassing both traditional and online avenues:

Businesses with no upfront cost:

For teenagers seeking to kickstart a business without financial constraints, options abound. Consider ventures like:

- **Childcare/babysitting**: Providing childcare services to neighbors or family friends during weekends or after school hours can generate extra income. Offering additional household chores while babysitting can enhance your service and set you apart.

- **Housekeeping**: Utilizing existing skills in household chores like cleaning, laundry, and organizing can translate into a profitable housekeeping business for teens.

- **Running errands**: If you have transportation, offering to run errands for busy individuals can be a lucrative endeavor. Services may include grocery shopping, post office runs, and other tasks.

- **Lawn care**: Mowing lawns for neighbors is a simple yet effective way to earn money. Borrowing a lawnmower initially minimizes startup costs.

- **Pet sitting or dog walking**: Catering to pet owners' needs by offering pet sitting or dog walking services can be rewarding, especially for animal lovers.

- **Car washing**: Providing car washing services, including exterior washing, interior vacuuming, and polishing, appeals to car owners seeking convenience.

Businesses with low-cost startup costs:

For teens willing to make a modest investment, several business opportunities exist:

- **Graphic or web design**: Capitalize on your tech skills by offering graphic or web design services to small businesses. Websites like WordPress and Wix offer free platforms to showcase your work initially.

- **Tutoring**: Sharing your knowledge by offering tutoring sessions to peers or younger students can be financially rewarding. Specialized skills like music or language tutoring can cater to a diverse clientele.

- **Selling items**: Utilize online platforms like eBay or Facebook Marketplace to sell handmade crafts or other items. Leverage personal social media accounts for additional promotion.

- **Blogging**: Starting a blog enables you to monetize your writing skills. Begin with free platforms like Google Sites or WordPress and explore affiliate link marketing for revenue generation.

Businesses with moderate upfront start-up costs:

Teenagers willing to invest substantially can explore business avenues such as:

- **Photography**: Invest in basic photography equipment to offer photography services for events or portraits.

- **Clothing resale**: Curate and sell thrift or vintage clothing items online or through pop-up shops.

- **Mobile car detailing**: Invest in car detailing equipment to offer comprehensive cleaning services at clients' locations.

By leveraging these business ideas, teens can embark on entrepreneurial journeys tailored to their interests and financial capacities, whether through traditional or online platforms.

Developing a Business Idea

Developing a viable business idea entails several crucial elements that ensure its success and sustainability. Here's a breakdown of how to generate a great business idea:

Identify clear demand:

Begin by recognizing a clear demand for a product or service. This involves observing consumer needs, and market trends, and identifying gaps in existing offerings. Your business idea is likely to resonate with customers and thrive if it addresses a genuine need.

Set short- and long-term goals:

Establish both short-term and long-term goals for your business idea. Short-term goals provide immediate direction and focus, while long-term goals outline the trajectory and vision for the business's growth and development.

Ensure room for growth:

Assess the scalability of your business idea. Ensure ample opportunity for growth and expansion in the chosen market or niche is possible. A business idea with potential for scalability allows for continuous evolution and adaptation to changing market dynamics.

Maintain motivation:

Sustain the right amount of motivation to drive your business idea forward. Passion and enthusiasm are vital for overcoming challenges and setbacks along the entrepreneurial journey. Cultivate a mindset of resilience and determination to see your idea through to fruition.

To develop your own business idea, consider the following approaches:

- **Invent a new product or service**: Brainstorm innovative solutions to address unmet needs or improve existing products or services. Focus on creating something unique and valuable that sets your business apart in the market.

- **Add value to an existing product**: Explore ways to enhance an existing product or service by improving its delivery, cost-effectiveness, customer experience, or other aspects. Adding value to an established offering can attract customers and differentiate your business.

- **innovate**: Embrace creativity and innovation to devise novel approaches to solving problems or fulfilling customer needs. Think outside the box and challenge conventional thinking to uncover innovative business ideas.

- **Jump on trend**: Stay abreast of current trends and emerging market opportunities. Identify trends that align with your interests and expertise. Capitalize on them by offering relevant products or services to meet evolving consumer preferences.

Generating a business idea requires creativity and insight into market demands. Here are some effective strategies to help you discover compelling business ideas:

Ask family and friends:

Tap into the insights of your close network. They offer unique perspectives and may identify business opportunities that align with your skills and interests. Additionally, their feedback can help you refine your ideas.

Consider problems in your everyday life:

Identify pain points or inefficiencies in your daily routine. These challenges present opportunities for innovative solutions. By addressing common problems, you can create a product or service that meets genuine needs in the market.

Build on your hobbies:

Leverage your passions and interests to inspire business ideas. Your hobbies can serve as a foundation for entrepreneurship, allowing you to pursue ventures that align with your interests and expertise.

Consider tasks you could make easier:

Explore ways to simplify existing processes or improve upon existing products or services. You can create value for customers and differentiate your business in the market by enhancing efficiency and convenience.

Build on existing products or services:

Look for gaps or areas of improvement in already existing products or services. By building upon existing offerings, you can capitalize on market demand while offering unique value propositions to customers.

Spend time on research:

Conduct thorough market research to identify emerging trends, unmet needs, and potential opportunities. This research provides valuable insights that inform your business idea and its implementation strategy.

By considering these key elements and approaches, aspiring entrepreneurs can develop compelling and viable business ideas that have the potential to succeed in today's dynamic marketplace. Remember to validate your idea through market research and careful planning before launching your venture.

Summary

In this chapter, we've dove into the essential process of identifying your passions and interests, emphasizing the significance of aligning these with your personal and professional endeavors. Armed with newfound clarity, you're poised to embark on a journey that resonates with your authentic self, driving motivation, satisfaction, and growth. As we transition to the next chapter, we'll shift our focus to the vital aspects of market research and understanding your target audience. By gaining actionable insights into consumer preferences, behaviors, and needs, you'll be equipped to make informed decisions about your product or service offerings. Get ready to explore the practical strategies that will empower you to tailor your offerings effectively, ensuring a successful venture that resonates with your audience.

Chapter 4
Conduct Market Research

Do a bit of research before you plan.
                                        –Kamaran Ihsan Salih

I N THE JOURNEY OF entrepreneurship, knowledge truly
is power. Before diving headfirst into the bustling marketplace, you must equip yourself with the necessary tools to
navigate the terrain effectively. Market research is the compass, guiding entrepreneurs toward success by providing invaluable insights into consumer preferences, behaviors, and
needs.

This chapter explores practical insights and actionable strategies for conducting comprehensive market research. By diving into the intricacies of understanding your target audience or market, you'll gain clarity to make informed decisions
about your product or service offerings. Through meticulous
analysis and strategic planning, you'll uncover hidden opportunities and identify potential pitfalls, empowering you to
chart a course toward sustainable growth and success. So, let's
roll up our sleeves and examine the art of market research,
where knowledge paves the way for prosperity.

Market Research

What exactly is market research, and why is it important for
startups? Let's unravel these questions and explore the intricacies of this essential process. Market research guides busi-

nesses through the seas of consumer behavior and economic trends. It involves gathering and analyzing data to understand the viability of a new product or service, defining target markets, and soliciting feedback from potential consumers:

Why is it important for startups?

Forecasts:

Market research provides invaluable insights for forecasting demand and anticipating market trends, enabling startups to prepare for future challenges and opportunities.

Competitive advantage:

Armed with market research findings, startups can carve out a competitive niche by identifying unmet needs, differentiating their offerings, and positioning themselves strategically in the marketplace.

Customer-centric:

By placing the spotlight on consumer preferences, behaviors, and pain points, market research empowers startups to tailor their products or services to meet the evolving needs of their target audience.

Valuable information:

Market research offers a treasure trove of information, illuminating market dynamics, competitor strategies, and emerging trends. It equips startups with the knowledge to make informed decisions and mitigate risks effectively.

How market research works:

Market research encompasses a spectrum of methodologies, from face-to-face interviews and focus groups to phone surveys and online research. Businesses leverage these tools to gather primary and secondary data, gaining a comprehensive understanding of consumer sentiments and market dynamics.

Types of Market Research

Face-to-face interviews: Traditional yet effective, face-to-face interviews enable researchers to engage directly with consumers, probing their preferences and opinions in a personalized manner.

Focus groups: Bringing together a select group of individuals, focus groups facilitate in-depth discussions and qualitative insights. This provides nuanced perspectives on product concepts and marketing strategies.

Phone research: While facing challenges in the digital age, phone research remains a viable option for gathering data efficiently and cost-effectively, providing valuable insights into consumer attitudes and behaviors.

Survey research: Surveys represent a versatile tool for gauging consumer opinions and preferences, offering quantitative data to inform decision-making and validate hypotheses.

Online market research: With the rise of digital platforms, online research is a popular choice. It enables businesses to reach a broader audience and collect data at scale while ensuring convenience and accessibility for participants.

Steps to Conduct Lean Market Research

Pursuing market research can feel daunting, but fear not. With a streamlined approach encompassing four key steps, you can unravel the mysteries of your target audience and gain invaluable insights into their desires and needs:

1. **Craft simple user personas**: User personas serve as your guiding stars in the vast cosmos of market research. Begin by outlining broad user categories, then dive deeper to segment your customer base and sculpt your ideal customer profile.

   ○ **Data gathering**: Harness the power of on-page or emailed surveys and interviews to discover the mysteries of your users and decipher what drives them to your business.

   ○ **Best practices**: Keep your survey concise, limiting questions to five or fewer to ensure thoughtful responses. Instead of fixating on typical demographics, focus on understanding users' roles and aspirations.

- ○ **Case study**: Take a leaf from Smallpdf's book. Through an on-page survey, they discovered that many users were administrative assistants, students, and teachers. Armed with this knowledge, they crafted simple user personas tailored to their distinct needs. Smallpdf is a versatile and all-in-one platform that allows you to convert and edit PDFs at no cost. You can complete tasks online by selecting a service from various options. Their professional team is here to assist you with their specialized web application.

2. **Engage in observational research**: Observe your users in their natural habitat to gain insights unfiltered by self-reporting biases. Whether overtly or covertly, watch how users interact with your product to uncover deeper understanding.

- ○ **Best practices**: Record observations diligently, noting each action and its context. Capture users' workflows comprehensively, delving into 'what,' 'why,' and 'for whom' of each interaction.

- ○ **Pitfalls to avoid**: Respect users' privacy and consent, by refraining from recording identifiable data without permission. Ensure transparency and clarity when requesting to observe users overtly, fostering cooperation and candid feedback.

- ○ **Case study**: Smallpdf took on both covert and overt observation studies. By discreetly observing students in cafes and libraries and openly engaging with administrative assistants, they unearthed valuable insights into user behaviors and pain points.

3. **Conduct individual interviews**: Forge meaningful connections with your target audience through one-on-one interviews. Dive deep into their thoughts, desires, and frustrations to unearth invaluable nuggets of wisdom.

- ○ **Best practices**: Adopt a listening-centric approach, allowing users to share their stories and insights freely. Channel your inner journalist, asking probing questions and refraining from leading or loaded inquiries.

- ○ **Pitfalls to avoid**: Steer clear of leading questions that betray bias and compromise respondents' honesty. Exercise caution when probing about future behaviors, mindful of cognitive biases skewing responses.

- ○ **Case study**: Smallpdf's journey led them to engage with university professors and administrative assistants through interviews. Although their initial focus shifted due to unforeseen circumstances, the lessons learned underscored the importance of agility in research endeavors.

Analyze the data (without drowning in it)

Wrap your head around the troves of data collected without becoming overwhelmed. Employ flow models and affinity diagrams to distill complex information into actionable insights.

Best practices: Visualize data flow through flow models, defining user interactions and pain points. Embrace affinity diagrams to categorize and synthesize large volumes of data, identifying overarching themes and patterns.

- **Pro tip**: Leverage tools like Hotjar's integrations to streamline data sharing and collaboration. Facilitate team engagement and analysis to derive meaningful insights from the data.

Armed with these steps, you're all set to go on a lean market research adventure, confidently understanding consumer preferences. Discover the valuable insights that help you make informed decisions and develop impactful strategies on your entrepreneurial journey.

Understanding Your Target Audience

Before jumping into the entrepreneurial space, conduct a thorough market analysis. This foundational step sets the stage for success, offering invaluable insights into your potential customers and the landscape in which you'll operate.

What Does Market Analysis Involve?

Market analysis is your compass in the vast ocean of business. It involves the process of engaging critical questions that guide your strategic decisions:

- Who are my prospects (customers)?

- What are the buying habits of my prospects?

- What is the size of my target market?

- What is the price my prospects are willing to pay?

- Who is my main competition?

- What are the strengths and weaknesses of my competition?

Benefits of Conducting a Market Analysis

Embracing market analysis yields a plethora of benefits, including:

- **Risk reduction**: Informed decisions mitigate potential pitfalls.

- **Emerging trends**: Stay ahead of the curve with insights into market shifts.

- **Targeted products or services**: Tailor offers to meet specific customer needs.

- **Evaluation benchmarks**: Measure performance against industry standards.

- **Revenue projections**: Gain clarity on potential earnings.

- **Marketing optimization**: Refine strategies for maximum impact.

- **Context for past mistakes**: Learn from previous missteps to chart a better course forward.

Challenges of Running a Market Analysis

While the rewards are plentiful, conducting a market analysis isn't without its hurdles:

- **Time-consuming**: Thorough research demands a significant time investment.

- **Costly**: Obtaining reliable data and insights may require financial resources.

- **Narrow focus**: It's easy to overlook broader market trends with a myopic view.

- **Need for extra staff**: Complex analyses may necessitate additional manpower.

How to Conduct a Market Analysis

Industry overview: Begin by understanding the broader landscape in which your business operates. Identify key players, market trends, and potential opportunities or threats.

Identify market gaps: Uncover unmet needs or underserved segments within your industry. These gaps present lucrative opportunities for innovation and differentiation.

Define your target market: Pinpoint specific demographic or psychographic characteristics of your ideal customers. Develop detailed buyer personas to guide your marketing efforts.

Investigate Competitors: Analyze the strengths, weaknesses, strategies, and market positioning of your competitors. Identify areas where you can differentiate and carve out a competitive advantage.

Identify barriers to entry: Assess potential obstacles that may impede your entry into the market. This could include regulatory hurdles, technological barriers, or entrenched competitors.

Create a sales forecast: Utilize market data and customer insights to project future sales figures. This forecast is a crucial tool for budgeting, resource allocation, and strategic planning.

Finding Your Target Audience

Finding your target audience is crucial for the success of your business. Here's a guide to help you through the customer analysis process:

What is a target audience?

Your target audience is the specific group of people most likely to be interested in and benefit from your product, service, or message. They share common characteristics, demographics, interests, or needs.

Benefits of Knowing Your Target Audience

Craft marketing strategies that work: Understanding your audience helps create impactful marketing campaigns.

Develop a winning brand identity: Knowing your audience allows you to create a brand identity that resonates with them.

Improve customer acquisition: Tailoring your marketing towards your audience makes it easier to acquire new customers.

Enhance customer satisfaction: Meeting the needs of your target audience leads to increased customer satisfaction.

Promote brand loyalty: Satisfied customers are more likely to remain loyal to your brand.

Types of Target Audiences

- **Purchase intention**: Consumers actively looking for a specific product or service.

- **Interests**: Consumers grouped based on hobbies, media consumption, or entertainment preferences.

- **Subculture**: Consumers categorized based on shared interests or affiliations.

5 Steps to Finding Your Target Audience

1. **Determine product/service characteristics**: Understand the problem your offering solves and who benefits from it.

2. **Research your market**: Analyze competitors to identify target audience characteristics and market gaps.

3. **Create buyer personas**: Develop profiles of imaginary people who represent your ideal customers.

4. **Consider marketing channels**: Determine where your target audience spends time and tailor your messaging accordingly.

5. **Test and refine**: Gather feedback, refine your target audience, and adjust your marketing strategies accordingly.

3 Target Audience Examples

New parents: Individuals or couples in their late 20s to early 40s, interested in parenting and childcare.

Tech enthusiasts: Predominantly younger individuals passionate about technology and innovation.

Sustainable living advocates: Environmentally conscious individuals across different age groups prioritize sustainable practices.

How to Reach Your Target Audience

- **Define your target audience**: Clearly define your target audience based on demographics, psychographics, and behaviors.

- **Do the research**: Conduct thorough market research to understand your audience's preferences and needs.

- **Use the right marketing channels**: Select effective marketing channels based on your audience's habits and preferences.

- **Tailor your messaging**: Craft personalized marketing messages that resonate with your target audience.

- **Continuously analyze and adapt**: Monitor campaign performance, gather feedback, and adapt your strategies to meet evolving consumer needs.

By following these steps, you effectively identify and reach your target audience, leading to increased engagement, loyalty, and business growth.

Building a Customer Persona

A buyer persona is a detailed profile of your ideal customer, crafted based on market research and audience insights. It includes demographic information, psychographic traits, behavior trends, values, desires, pain points, and affiliations:

Buyer personas are crucial for several reasons:

Informing product development: By understanding your customers deeply, you can tailor your products or services to meet their needs effectively.

Personalizing marketing: Buyer personas help you create targeted marketing campaigns that resonate with specific segments of your audience, increasing engagement and conversion rates.

Optimizing demand generation: With detailed buyer personas, you can optimize your demand generation, lead generation, and lead nurturing strategies to attract high-value customers effectively.

Tailoring product messaging: Buyer personas enable you to craft messaging that speaks directly to your target audience, increasing the relevance and effectiveness of your communication.

In marketing, buyer's personas are utilized in various ways:

- **Guiding product development**: Understanding customer needs and preferences informs product or service enhancements.

- **Informing content generation**: Buyer personas help tailor content to address specific pain points and interests of different customer segments.

- **Enhancing lead follow-up**: With insights into customer preferences, sales teams can tailor their approach to effectively nurture leads.

- **Improving customer acquisition and retention**: Targeted marketing efforts based on buyer personas lead to better acquisition and retention rates.

Common buyer personas include those representing Gen Z and Gen X demographics, each with distinct characteristics and preferences. Other examples include:

- Stay-at-home moms with young children

- Men who work in manual labor jobs and are football fans

- Retirees who travel frequently but are on a budget

- Families with children camp frequently

To create a buyer persona, follow these four steps:

1. **Gather basic demographic information**: Collect data on age, gender, location, education, job title, industry, income, and other relevant demographic factors.

2. **Understand motivations**: Dive deep into your persona's motivations, desires, pain points, and challenges to understand what drives their purchasing decisions.

3. **Prepare your sales team**: Equip your sales team with insights into the persona's needs, preferences, and pain points to facilitate more meaningful conversations.

4. **Craft targeted messaging**: Develop messaging that resonates with your persona, addressing their specific needs and interests in a language they understand.

By involving stakeholders from marketing, sales, customer service, product development, and management, you ensure diverse perspectives are considered in the persona creation process.

Creating Minimum Viable Product (MVP)

Minimum Viable Product (MVP) is the initial version of a product that includes only the essential features necessary to address core questions about its viability in the market. This approach allows startups to validate assumptions quickly and cost-effectively, which is crucial in the lean startup methodology. By starting with an MVP, founders can mitigate the risk of failure by testing the market's reaction to their solution before investing resources in a fully-fledged product.

Building an MVP involves several key steps:

1. **Create a problem statement**: Identify the problem your product aims to solve. This can be done by leveraging domain expertise, dissatisfaction with existing solutions, or validating externally identified problems.

2. **Conduct market research**: Analyze the market to ensure there is demand for your solution. Explore competitors, identify the target audience, and assess the market size to validate the need for your product.

3. **Prototype the potential solution**: Create a prototype to visualize the solution and validate the User Interface (UI) and user Experience (UX) design. Prototyping helps gather early feedback for improvements before moving to MVP development.

4. **Define the list of features**: Prioritize essential features to prevent feature creep and maintain focus on solving the core problem. Use frameworks like story mapping to organize features based on usage sequence and importance.

5. **Develop your MVP**: Build the MVP with a balance between professionalism and simplicity. Ensure the MVP is bug-free and of high quality to allow users to experience the core value of the product.

6. **Get user feedback and repeat**: Collect feedback from users to refine the MVP further. Incorporate user insights to improve the product and validate its market fit through constant iteration.

7. **Measure success**: Evaluate the success of the MVP by analyzing key metrics such as user engagement, retention rates, and conversion rates. Adjust strategies based on the gathered data to optimize the product's performance.

After launching an MVP, it's essential to continue iterating based on user feedback to enhance the product further. Different types of MVPs, such as landing page MVPs, pre-order MVPs, single-feature MVPs, concierge MVPs, and Wizard of Oz MVPs, offer varying approaches to validating product ideas based on specific business needs. The cost of MVP development varies depending on factors like features, scope, and complexity. Some products will cost less to develop, while others could cost much more. However, it's crucial to focus on delivering value through integral features rather than striving for perfectionism, which can lead to unnecessary delays and costs. Overcoming common challenges like lack of clear focus, feature creep, perfectionism, and neglecting user feedback requires setting SMART goals, prioritizing core features, and establishing a feedback loop to continuously gather insights for refinement.

Summary

In this chapter, we dove into the critical process of market research and understanding your target audience, offering actionable strategies to help entrepreneurs make informed decisions about their product or service offerings. By gaining insights into consumer preferences, behaviors, and needs, entrepreneurs can effectively tailor their offerings to meet market demands. Key takeaways include the importance of validating assumptions, conducting thorough market analysis, and continuously gathering feedback to refine offerings and optimize market fit.

Now, armed with a deep understanding of the audience and market landscape, you are ready to take the next step. In the following chapter, I will guide you through the process of developing a comprehensive business plan. This essential document not only communicates your vision but also attracts stakeholders and sets the groundwork for success. From outlining business objectives to crafting financial projections, the next chapter will provide step-by-step guidance to empower you to chart a course for success. Get ready to transform your vision into a concrete roadmap for growth and prosperity!

Chapter 5
Creating a Winning Business Plan

A goal without a plan is just a wish.
> −Antoine de Saint-Exupéry

I N THE TURBULENT SPHERE of entrepreneurship, dreams drive innovation and fuel progress. Entrepreneurs pave the path to success with meticulous planning and strategic foresight. Every entrepreneur has a vision burning in their hearts, but without a roadmap to guide their steps, that vision risks remaining a mere aspiration.

This chapter empowers entrepreneurs and provides clarity as they navigate the intricate landscape of business development. With step-by-step guidance, I'll unveil the art and science of crafting a robust business plan. The blueprint presented here not only articulates the entrepreneur's vision but also entices stakeholders to collaborate in their quest for success.

Defining objectives, outlining strategies, analyzing the market, and projecting financial forecasts are all integral components of a business plan. Each serves as a cornerstone for entrepreneurial ventures. With meticulous planning and strategic alignment, entrepreneurs transform their dreams into tangible realities, laying the groundwork for sustainable growth and prosperity.

Join me on this empowering adventure, where vision meets strategy, and dreams take flight through thoughtful planning. Together, we will unlock the potential within, harness the power of purpose, and chart a course towards entrepreneurial success.

The Business Plan

The business plan is like a map that helps entrepreneurs bring their visions to life. But what exactly is a business plan, and what does it entail? Simply put, a business plan is a comprehensive document outlining a company's goals and the strategies it intends to employ to achieve them. Whether it's a startup seeking to attract investors or an established enterprise aiming to stay focused on its objectives, a well-crafted business plan is indispensable.

So, what components make up a business plan?

Let's break it down:

- **Executive summary**: This section provides an overview of the company, including its mission, leadership, operations, and key locations.

- **Products and services**: Here, the company details its offerings, including pricing, unique benefits, production processes, patents, and research and development efforts.

- **Market analysis**: Understanding the industry landscape is crucial. This section delves into market dynamics, competition, target customers, and strategies to capture market share.

- **Marketing strategy**: This section outlines marketing campaigns, distribution channels, and promotional activities.

- **Financial plans and projections**: Whether it's presenting financial statements for established businesses or setting targets for new ventures, this section covers financial forecasts and funding requests.

While business plans may vary in length and format, they typically include these core elements. And while there's no one-size-fits-all approach, a compelling business plan showcases the company's uniqueness and potential for success.

The Purpose of a Business Plan

The purpose of a business plan extends far beyond being just a document; it's the foundation of entrepreneurial success. Here's why every aspiring business owner should prioritize crafting a comprehensive business plan:

Prove your idea is viable:

Before rushing into entrepreneurship, a business plan allows you to thoroughly assess the viability of your idea. Market research and competitor analysis allow you to determine if there's a demand for your product or service.

Set important goals:

A business plan isn't just about the present; it's about envisioning the future. It enables you to set both short-term and long-term goals, providing a roadmap for the growth and development of your business.

Reduce potential risks:

Entrepreneurship inherently involves risks, but a well-thought-out business plan helps mitigate them. You're better prepared to navigate unforeseen obstacles by identifying potential challenges and developing contingency plans.

Build your team:

A compelling business plan not only attracts investors but also top-tier talent. It outlines your vision for the company and clarifies roles and responsibilities, making it easier to recruit and onboard the right team members.

Allocate resources and plan purchases:

From product development to marketing initiatives, a business plan helps budget resources effectively. By outlining your financial projections and investment needs, you can make informed decisions about resource allocation and funding.

Share your vision:

Your business plan is the blueprint for your company's future. It articulates your vision to stakeholders, including investors, employees, and partners. It aligns everyone towards a common goal and fosters a sense of collective ownership.

Develop a marketing strategy:

A robust marketing strategy is essential for brand awareness and customer acquisition. Within your business plan, you can outline your target market, value proposition, and advertising tactics, laying the foundation for successful marketing campaigns.

Focus your energy:

In the fast-paced world of entrepreneurship, it's easy to get distracted by competing priorities. A business plan helps you stay focused by identifying key priorities, and ensuring your efforts are aligned with your business objectives.

Top Tips for Writing a Business Plan

By following these tips and tailoring them to your specific business needs, you can create a compelling business plan that sets the stage for entrepreneurial success. Here are expert tips to craft a winning business plan:

Keep it simple and focused:

Avoid overwhelming your readers with lengthy documents. Choose a clear, concise format that highlights your goals and strategies. Use readable fonts and a clean layout to enhance readability and comprehension.

Conduct thorough market research:

Investigate your industry, target audience, and competitors. Gather data on market size, trends, and consumer preferences to inform your business decisions and validate your strategies.

Set realistic financial projections:

Develop comprehensive financial forecasts that project revenue, expenses, and cash flow. Ensure your projections are realistic and supported by thorough research and analysis.

Define your operational processes:

Clearly outline how your business will operate, from production and inventory management to staffing and distribution. Establish efficient processes to ensure consistency and quality in your operations.

Create a strong marketing plan:

Craft a robust marketing strategy that identifies your target audience, analyzes competitors, and outlines marketing channels and tactics. Embrace market research to understand your competitive landscape and position your business for success.

Address legal and regulatory considerations:

Navigate the legal and regulatory requirements relevant to your industry and business structure. Detail how your business will comply with these regulations to mitigate risks and ensure compliance.

Plan for scalability and growth:

Anticipate future growth opportunities and outline strategies for scaling your business. Develop scalable processes and infrastructure to support expansion while maintaining operational efficiency.

Include an exit strategy:

Prepare for the future by outlining potential exit strategies, such as mergers, acquisitions, or IPOs. This demonstrates to investors that you have a long-term vision for your business and are prepared for various outcomes.

How to Write a Business Plan

Crafting a business plan from scratch can feel daunting, but breaking it down into manageable steps makes the process much more straightforward. Here's a step-by-step guide to help you create a comprehensive business plan:

1. **Draft an executive summary**: This section provides a high-level overview of your business. Include key points such as your business concept, goals, products/services, target market, marketing strategy, financial status, and team composition. Keep it concise yet compelling.

2. **Write a company description**: Describe your business, its structure, industry, vision, mission, value proposition, history, and objectives. Clearly articulate what sets your business apart and why it's a good investment.

3. **Provide a market analysis**: Summarize your target market, industry trends, competitors, and potential growth opportunities. Describe insights into market size, consumer behavior, SWOT analysis, and the competitive landscape to validate your business idea.

4. **Outline the management and organization**: Detail the legal structure of your business and introduce key personnel. Use organizational charts to illustrate

roles, responsibilities, and relationships within your team.

5. **List your products and services**: Describe your offerings, their unique features and benefits, and how they fulfill customer needs. Highlight any intellectual property or future product plans.

6. **Perform customer segmentation**: Define your ideal customer profile by demographics, behaviors, preferences, and needs. Tailor your marketing efforts to resonate with your target audience effectively.

7. **Define a marketing plan**: Develop a comprehensive marketing strategy that covers pricing, product positioning, promotion, and distribution channels. Align your marketing tactics with your target market and business goals.

8. **Provide a logistics and operations plan**: Outline the logistical workflows, suppliers, production processes, facilities, equipment, shipping, inventory management, and contingency plans.

9. **Make a financial plan**: Create detailed financial projections, including income statements, balance sheets, cash flow statements, and break-even analysis. Estimate startup costs, revenue streams, expenses, and funding requirements accurately.

10. **Add additional information in an appendix**: Include supplementary materials like resumes, market research data, legal documents, contracts, and any other relevant information that supports your business plan.

Remember, your business plan should be tailored to your specific business goals, audience, and industry. It's a dynamic document that should evolve as your business grows and circumstances change. By following these steps and leveraging business plan templates or software, you can create a robust roadmap for your business's success.

The Reasons Why Business Plans Fail

Business plans can face a multitude of challenges that can lead to failure. These range from fundamental flaws in the business idea to more nuanced issues like ineffective team dynamics. Let's review the reasons why business plans often falter and explore strategies to avoid these pitfalls:

Bad Business Ideas:

Many failed business plans are the result of flawed or untested business ideas. While an idea may seem promising initially, it's essential to validate it through methods like user-driven development (UDD). By engaging with potential customers early on, businesses can gauge market demand and adjust their offerings accordingly. This iterative approach, exemplified by Stanford University's D-School, involves gathering user feedback to refine products and ensure alignment with market needs.

Employee compensation misalignment:

Incentive compatibility is crucial for ensuring employee goals align with company objectives. If compensation structures incentivize short-term gains over long-term success, employees may prioritize individual interests over organizational goals. Tailoring compensation packages to individual preferences and incorporating long-term incentives can help foster alignment between employee and company objectives.

Lack of exit strategy for handling team conflicts:

Team conflicts are inevitable in any business venture, making it essential to have clear procedures for resolving disputes. Assigning specific roles and responsibilities to each co-founder, along with established consequences for non-compliance, can mitigate conflicts. Additionally, conducting thorough due diligence when selecting co-founders and delineating roles can prevent potential conflicts from arising.

Imbalanced team composition:

A well-balanced team is crucial for executing a business plan effectively. Many plans falter due to a lack of diversity or expertise within the team. A competent team possessing the necessary skills is essential for attracting investors and fostering success.

Incomplete financial projections:

Detailed financial projections are often overlooked but are critical for demonstrating the feasibility and profitability of a business venture. Balance sheets, cash flow statements, and profit and loss statements provide essential insights into the company's financial health and prospects. Utilizing tools like business calculators aids in generating accurate financial forecasts and bolsters the credibility of the business plan.

Spelling and grammar errors:

Poorly edited business plans can undermine credibility and professionalism, leading to investor disinterest. Employing professional editors to review the plan for spelling and grammar mistakes can enhance readability and convey competence to potential investors.

False assumptions:

Making assumptions about investor preferences or market sentiments without proper research can prove detrimental. Conducting thorough research and avoiding controversial or unfounded assumptions can help mitigate risks and ensure alignment with stakeholders' values.

Failure to incorporate feedback:

Neglecting to reassess and improve the business plan based on feedback can hinder its effectiveness. Soliciting input from advisors and stakeholders and incorporating constructive criticism can strengthen the plan and increase its chances of success.

By addressing these common pitfalls and adopting proactive strategies, businesses can enhance the quality and effectiveness of their business plans, increasing their likelihood of attracting investment and achieving success.

Summary

As we conclude this chapter, you now possess the tools to craft a compelling business plan that embodies your vision and captivates stakeholders. Follow the step-by-step guidance to lay the groundwork for success, setting the stage for your entrepreneurial journey.

Key takeaways from this chapter include the importance of structuring your business plan effectively, tailoring the content to resonate with your audience, and leveraging sample plans as reference materials. Additionally, you've learned how to communicate your value proposition, analyze market trends, and project financial performance with confidence and clarity.

Transitioning to the next chapter, the focus shifts to the critical aspect of securing funding for your venture and mastering the principles of money management. The goal is to empower you with the knowledge and strategies necessary to navigate complex funding options while also instilling essential principles of budgeting, financial planning, and resource allocation.

Throughout the upcoming chapter, you can expect to explore various funding avenues available to entrepreneurs, ranging from traditional loans and venture capital to crowdfunding and bootstrapping. We'll dive into the fundamentals of budgeting, helping you optimize your financial resources and make informed decisions that drive sustainable growth and profitability.

Prepare to embark on a journey that demystifies the world of entrepreneurial finance, equipping you with the tools and insights needed to fuel your venture's success. Get ready to unlock the secrets of securing funding and mastering money management as we move into the next chapter.

Chapter 6
Mastering Funding and Financial Foundations

In business, you don't get what you deserve, you get what you negotiate.

–John Mariotti

T HE WORDS ABOVE FROM the president of "The Enterprise Group" encapsulate a fundamental truth of
entrepreneurship: success often hinges on navigating negotiations effectively.

Entrepreneurs who approach funding opportunities with
diligence, assertiveness, and strategic prowess are better positioned to secure the resources they need to fuel their growth.
I invite you to the gateway of financial empowerment. In
this chapter, we unlock the secrets of funding and money
management for entrepreneurs.

The first step in our journey is realizing that securing funding
involves more than just making a request. It's about negotiating terms that align with your business objectives and growth
trajectory. This chapter delves into the wide range of funding
options entrepreneurs can choose from, such as traditional loans, venture capital, crowdfunding, and bootstrapping.
But our exploration doesn't end there. We will explore the
fundamental concepts of budgeting, financial planning, and
resource allocation. These skills are essential for fostering sustainable growth and achieving success.

By the end of this chapter, you'll have the knowledge and
strategies necessary to navigate the complex terrain of fund-

ing negotiations and financial management. So, let's embark on this journey together, empowering you to realize your entrepreneurial vision and achieve lasting success in the dynamic business world.

Funding Your Business

Every entrepreneur inevitably encounters the hurdle of funding. Whether launching a startup or scaling an existing venture, securing financial resources is crucial for success. But navigating the landscape of funding options can be daunting, especially for those unfamiliar with the terrain. However, I'm here to illuminate the path forward:

Crowdfunding:

Crowdfunding platforms like GoFundMe offer a democratized approach to fundraising, allowing entrepreneurs to leverage the collective support of individuals worldwide. Craft a compelling campaign, tap into your network, and showcase your passion to attract backers. Remember, friends and family can be your strongest allies in this endeavor.

Angel investors:

Angel investors, often seasoned entrepreneurs, provide capital in exchange for equity or convertible debt. Their financial backing coupled with strategic guidance can catapult growth for early-stage startups. To capture their interest, cultivate relationships, refine your pitch, and demonstrate the scalability of your venture.

Bootstrapping:

For those averse to relinquishing ownership, bootstrapping offers a self-reliant path to funding. Tap into personal savings, liquidate assets, or explore alternative financing options like microloans. While bootstrapping requires resourcefulness and resilience, it empowers entrepreneurs to retain control and autonomy over their vision.

Venture capitalists (VCs):

VCs specialize in financing high-growth startups with transformative potential. Pitching to VCs demands precision and clarity, highlighting market opportunity, traction, and scalability. While VC funding may entail equity dilution, it provides access to capital, expertise, and invaluable network connections.

Microloans:

Microloans offer accessible financing solutions for budding entrepreneurs, particularly those underserved by traditional banking institutions. Explore microfinance organizations and community lenders who offer flexible terms and tailored support. Remember, meticulous financial planning is essential to ensuring repayment feasibility.

Small Business Administration (SBA):

Navigating Government Assistance Government programs administered by the SBA provides a lifeline for entrepreneurs seeking funding. From grants to loan guarantees, SBA initiatives offer financial support and educational resources to fuel business growth. However, competition can be fierce, so meticulous preparation is paramount.

Best Practices for Successful Fundraising

- **Practice due diligence**: Conduct thorough research and scrutiny before engaging in any fundraising arrangement, safeguarding your interests and mitigating risks.

- **Organize bookkeeping**: Maintain meticulous financial records to instill confidence in potential investors and lenders, showcasing transparency and accountability.

- **Refine your pitch**: Articulate a compelling value proposition, emphasizing impact, scalability, and differentiation to captivate stakeholders' attention.

- **Embrace creativity**: Explore unconventional fundraising avenues, leveraging contests, product pre-sales, and strategic partnerships to diversify funding sources.

- **Share your enthusiasm**: Infuse your fundraising efforts with passion and conviction, rallying supporters around your vision and fostering a sense of collective ownership.

Pitching Your Business Ideas to Win Investors

Pitching your business idea to potential investors can be the pivotal moment that propels your entrepreneurial journey forward. It's an opportunity to transform your vision into reality by securing the funding and support needed to bring your ideas to life. But crafting a compelling pitch requires more than a good idea—it demands a strategic approach and effective communication. In this section, I'll walk you through the essential steps to master the art of pitching your business ideas and winning over investors:

Craft your elevator pitch

Your elevator pitch is your gateway to capturing investors' attention in a concise and impactful manner. In just 30 seconds, distill your business idea into a clear and compelling message highlighting its uniqueness and value proposition. Use this pitch not only as an introduction but also as guidance throughout your presentation.

Know your audience

Tailor your pitch to resonate with your audience by understanding their backgrounds, interests, and motivations. Conduct thorough research to uncover insights that enable you to customize your message effectively. Whether pitching to financial backers or industry experts, align your presentation to address their specific needs and concerns.

Tailor your pitch

Personalize your pitch to address the challenges and aspirations of your audience. Beyond showcasing the features of your business idea, focus on articulating how it addresses their pain points and offers tangible solutions. Establishing a personal connection through your pitch can foster genuine interest and engagement from potential investors.

Create your pitch deck

Craft a visually compelling pitch deck to complement your verbal presentation. Your pitch deck should provide a comprehensive overview of your business idea, emphasizing key points and supporting data. Consider creating two versions—a concise deck for presentations and a more detailed one for further reading.

Tell a compelling story

Harness the power of storytelling to captivate your audience and illustrate the relevance of your business idea. Craft a narrative highlighting the problem your idea solves and the journey that led to its inception. By weaving a compelling story, you can evoke emotions and resonate with your audience on a deeper level.

Demonstrate your solution

Articulate how your business idea addresses the identified problem and delivers value to your target customers. Highlight the key benefits of your product or service and emphasize its unique selling points. Your value proposition should be clear and compelling, showcasing why your solution is the best choice and solves the problem.

Identify your target market

Define your target market and quantify the potential opportunity it represents. Develop a detailed profile of your ideal customers and estimate the size of your target market segments. By demonstrating a clear understanding of your market dynamics, you can instill confidence in investors regarding the scalability and viability of your business idea.

Describe your business model

Outline your business model to explain how your company generates revenue and creates value. Provide insights into your operations, distribution channels, and revenue streams. Investors need assurance that your business model is sustainable and capable of long-term growth and profitability.

Showcase your competitive advantage

Highlight what sets your business apart and position it for success. Conduct a competitive analysis to identify your strengths and weaknesses relative to rival offerings. Utilize visuals, such as comparison charts, to illustrate your competitive edge and reinforce your value proposition.

Highlight your successes and traction

Demonstrate tangible evidence of your business's achievements and milestones to bolster credibility. Provide metrics such as sales numbers, customer testimonials, and strategic partnerships. By showcasing your track record of success, you instill confidence in investors and validate the potential of your business idea.

Provide financial projections

Offer investors a glimpse into the future by presenting realistic financial projections. Base your projections on sound data and market insights, outlining your revenue forecasts and growth trajectory. Transparency and accuracy are paramount, as investors rely on financial projections to assess the investment potential of your business.

Explain the customer acquisition process

Detail your strategy for acquiring and retaining customers, highlighting your marketing tactics and customer acquisition costs. Showcase your understanding of customer acquisition channels and demonstrate how you plan to leverage them to drive growth. Clarity and specificity are essential to instilling confidence in investors regarding your go-to-market strategy.

Introduce your team

Introduce the key members of your team and their respective roles, emphasizing their expertise and contributions. Investors fund people as much as they do ideas, so highlight the strengths and capabilities of your team members. Building rapport and trust with potential investors starts with showcasing the talent and dedication of your team.

Declare your funding needs

Clearly articulate your funding requirements and the specific investment or partnership opportunities you're seeking. Provide details on existing investments, ownership structure, and the allocation of funds. Transparency about your financial needs and objectives enables investors to make informed decisions aligned with their investment criteria.

Address audience questions

Allocate time for questions and feedback from your audience, demonstrating openness and receptiveness to their input. Anticipate common questions, and prepare thoughtful responses to address them effectively. Engaging in constructive dialogue fosters trust and collaboration, laying the groundwork for a productive partnership.

Prepare for objections

Anticipate potential objections or concerns investors may raise during your pitch and develop persuasive rebuttals.

Maintain composure and confidence in addressing objections, reframing them as opportunities for clarification and reassurance. Demonstrate resilience and credibility with honesty and transparency in acknowledging challenges.

Solicit feedback

Seek feedback from investors and stakeholders following your pitch. Leverage their insights to refine and improve your presentation. Express gratitude for their time and input, demonstrating a commitment to continuous learning and growth. Incorporating feedback strengthens your pitch and enhances your ability to resonate with future audiences.

Practice, practice, practice

Rehearse your pitch rigorously to refine your delivery and enhance your confidence. Practice articulating key points, responding to questions, and navigating potential challenges seamlessly. Solicit feedback from peers and mentors, incorporating their perspectives to fine-tune your presentation. With each iteration, you'll sharpen your pitch and increase your chances of success.

Mastering the art of pitching your business ideas to investors requires preparation, persuasion, and persistence. By following these steps and honing your pitching skills, you'll be well-equipped to seize opportunities, secure funding, and bring your entrepreneurial aspirations to fruition. So, step into the spotlight, showcase your vision, and let your passion for innovation shine brightly.

Establishing a Strong Financial Foundation for Your Business

Navigating the complexities of financial management is a critical aspect of ensuring the success and longevity of your venture. From overseeing day-to-day expenses to planning for future growth, effective money management is key. This section explores essential areas every business owner should master to maintain a healthy financial pulse.

Budgeting

Budgeting is the roadmap for businesses, guiding spending decisions and financial planning. By assessing expected income and expenses, you can set clear financial targets and track performance against these goals. Business owners can create realistic budgets that align with their growth objectives by utilizing historical data and market insights.

Cash flow management

Managing cash flow is crucial for maintaining liquidity and ensuring operational stability. Understanding the timing of income and expenses, maintaining cash reserves, and forecasting future cash flow are essential strategies. Additionally, effectively managing accounts receivable and payable optimizes cash flow and supports ongoing business activities.

Tax planning and compliance

Tax planning is integral to minimizing liabilities and ensuring compliance with tax laws. Businesses can optimize their tax strategies by staying informed about deadlines, rate changes, and deductions. Seeking guidance from tax professionals provides valuable insight and peace of mind in navigating complex tax regulations.

Banking

Choosing the right banking products and services can streamline financial operations and enhance efficiency. Business checking and savings accounts, remote deposit capture, and fraud mitigation tools are essential for managing cash flow and protecting against financial risks. Credit lines and merchant services offer flexible financing options and facilitate customer transactions.

Debts

Understanding and managing debts is essential for maintaining financial health. Whether through traditional bank loans or alternative funding sources, businesses must evaluate the impact of debt on their financial strategy. Proper debt management involves assessing repayment terms, interest rates, and overall borrowing capacity.

Tracking key metrics and ratios

Monitoring key performance indicators (KPIs) and financial ratios provides valuable insights into business performance. Metrics such as net profit margin, accounts receivable turnover, and inventory turnover enable business owners to assess profitability, efficiency, and liquidity. Regular reviews empower entrepreneurs to make informed decisions and adapt strategies as needed.

Tips for Managing Business Finances

Here are some tips for effectively managing your business finances:

- Ensure you're paying yourself a consistent salary. Even if it's a modest amount, this practice helps you cover personal expenses and build personal savings, ensuring financial stability beyond the business.

- Maintain a clear separation between your personal and business finances. Opening a dedicated business bank account helps you track expenses accurately and provides proper documentation for tax deductions, safeguarding against potential issues during audits.

- Start by organizing the essential financial documents required for effective management. These documents include:

- *The balance sheet*, which reflects your business's assets, liabilities, and equity

- *Profit and loss statement*, detailing revenue, expenses, and profitability over a defined period

- *Cash flow statement*, summarizing cash movement in and out of the business.

- Stay vigilant about deadlines related to taxes, payments, and financial reporting. Missing deadlines can lead to penalties and disruptions in cash flow, potentially harming your business's financial health.

- Monitor your business spending closely to identify areas where costs can be optimized or reduced. Regularly reviewing expenses helps maintain financial discipline and ensures resources are allocated efficiently.

- Adhere to accounting best practices to maintain accurate financial records. Choosing between cash and accrual-basis accounting depends on your business's needs and complexities. Implementing accounting software streamlines financial tracking and reporting, enhancing efficiency and accuracy.

- Consider seeking professional accounting assistance, especially as your business grows. Accounting professionals provide strategic advice, help with business planning, and manage complex financial tasks, ensuring compliance and optimal financial performance.

Creating Your Business Budget

Here are some fundamental principles for creating and managing your business budget effectively:

List all expenses

Identify and categorize all business expenses, including rent, employee salaries, supplies, and services, to understand your daily and monthly operating costs. Creating both short-term and long-term projections with your income helps with financial planning.

Budget for growth

Allocate funds for business improvements and expansion initiatives, ensuring they are prioritized and funded without accumulating debt unnecessarily. Saving for future growth enhances long-term financial health and provides security for your business and family.

Anticipate business income

Understand your expected business income each month to facilitate effective budget allocation and financial planning. Predictable income streams enable you to allocate resources strategically and manage expenses efficiently.

Establish savings goals

Set aside funds regularly for business expansion or emergencies to maintain financial stability and support growth. Saving from the outset helps build a financial cushion for challenging periods and ensures resilience against unexpected setbacks.

Identify cost-cutting opportunities

Regularly review your expenses to identify areas where costs can be reduced without compromising quality. Efficiency and frugality are essential for sustainable business success, and trimming unnecessary expenses enhances profitability.

Maintain realistic expectations

Set realistic expectations for income and expenses based on thorough research and market analysis. Avoid expanding too quickly and ensure your budget reflects achievable goals and growth projections.

Adhering to these budgeting basics allows small business owners to establish a solid financial foundation, maximize efficiency, and achieve their business goals effectively. Keeping personal and business finances separate, setting clear savings goals, and regularly evaluating expenses are key to financial success.

Components of a Business Budget

Here's a breakdown of the key elements of a business budget
and how they apply to various types of companies:

- **Fixed costs**: These are consistent expenses like rent,
  utilities, insurance, and salaries that don't vary with
  sales volume. They provide a baseline for your budget and should be accounted for regardless of your
  business activity.

- **Estimated revenue**: This represents the income you
  expect to generate from sales of goods or services.
  It's crucial for planning your budget and allocating
  resources effectively.

- **Cash flow**: Cash flow tracks the movement of money into and out of your business over a specific period. Having enough liquidity to cover expenses and
  manage day-to-day operations is essential.

- **Variable costs**: Variable costs fluctuate with sales
  volume or production levels. These expenses include
  items such as raw materials, inventory, shipping, and
  sales commissions. Monitoring and budgeting for
  variable costs are vital for maintaining profitability.

- **Profit**: Profit is what remains after deducting expenses from revenue. It's a key indicator of business
  performance and sustainability. Budgeting for profit

helps set financial goals and measure success.

- **One-off costs**: These are occasional or non-recurring expenses such as equipment purchases, office relocations, or marketing campaigns. While not part of regular operations, they should be accounted for in your budget to avoid unexpected financial strain.

Small Business Budgets for Different Types of Company

Seasonal businesses

Seasonal businesses experience fluctuations in demand and revenue throughout the year. Budgeting helps them anticipate slow periods, manage cash flow effectively, and plan for peak seasons.

Inventory businesses

Inventory-based businesses must budget for stocking up on inventory to meet demand. They must balance inventory levels with sales forecasts to optimize cash flow and minimize carrying costs.

Start-ups

Start-ups face unique budgeting challenges due to uncertainty and limited historical data. They must research industry benchmarks, plan for various expenses like salaries and marketing, and allocate resources strategically to support growth.

E-commerce businesses

E-commerce businesses must consider factors like shipping costs, web hosting, online marketing, and product photography in their budgets. They must budget for a seamless online shopping experience while managing expenses effectively.

Creating a comprehensive budget tailored to your business type helps you make informed decisions, manage resources efficiently, and achieve financial goals. By understanding and prioritizing different budget components, businesses can navigate economic challenges and plan for long-term success.

Creating a Business Budget in Easy Steps

Crafting a business budget is crucial to the success and sustainability of your small business. Here are some simplified steps to help you navigate the process effectively:

1. **Assess your business needs**: Before diving into budgeting, take the time to identify areas for improvement within your business. This will help you determine where your funds should be allocated. Whether paying off debts, investing in new equipment, or setting aside funds for marketing, knowing your priorities is key to effective budgeting.

2. **Set clear goals**: Establish short-term and long-term goals for your business, being mindful of your incoming and outgoing cash flow. Short-term goals

may include debt repayment or equipment purchases, while long-term goals could involve marketing expenses to support overall growth.

3. **Analyze costs**: Thoroughly research and understand all operating costs associated with your business. This includes fixed expenses like rent, utilities, and insurance, as well as variable costs such as labor commissions. Overestimating costs can provide a buffer for unexpected expenses, ensuring financial stability.

4. **Negotiate with suppliers**: If your business relies on suppliers, consider negotiating discounted rates for materials or services. Building strong relationships with suppliers can lead to flexible payment terms and potential cost savings, particularly during periods of low cash flow.

5. **Estimate revenue realistically**: Avoid the pitfall of overestimating revenue by analyzing past sales data. Use previous revenue figures as a reference point for setting realistic goals. This empirical approach ensures that your budget aligns with your business's capacity to generate income.

6. **Understand gross profit margin**: Gain insight into your business's financial health by calculating your gross profit margin. This metric reflects the dif-

ference between revenue and expenses, highlighting areas for cost reduction or revenue enhancement. A thorough understanding of your gross profit margin is essential for effective budgeting.

7. **Project cash flow**: Balance customer and vendor payments to maintain a steady cash flow within your organization. Implement flexible payment terms for customers while setting aside funds for potential late payments or bad debt. Allocating cash flow effectively ensures timely payment of expenses and supports business initiatives.

8. **Consider seasonal and industry trends**: Anticipate fluctuations in revenue due to seasonal variations or industry trends. Allocate resources strategically to sustain your business during slower periods and capitalize on peak seasons. Understanding market dynamics helps mitigate financial risks and ensures long-term viability.

9. **Set spending goals**: Evaluate spending priorities to optimize resource allocation. Identify areas where expenses can be reduced or redirected to support business objectives. Wisely investing in initiatives that contribute to long-term growth is essential for budget success.

10. **Consolidate your budget**: Compile all the gath-

ered information to create a comprehensive budget for your business. Subtract fixed and variable expenses from projected income to determine available funds. Prepare for unexpected expenses by setting aside reserves, and adjust your budget as needed to achieve short-term and long-term goals.

Role of Accounting Software

Utilize accounting software to streamline budgeting processes and access real-time financial data. Accounting systems provide insights into costs, revenue, and cash flow, facilitating informed decision-making. Regularly compare budget projections with actual performance to evaluate budget effectiveness and make necessary adjustments.

Business Budget Template

Use this template to monitor your business's financial performance and make informed decisions to ensure the financial health and success of your company. Adjust budgeted amounts and analyze actual expenses to stay on track with your financial goals:

Item	Description	Budgeted Amount	Actual Amount	Over/Under
Labor hours	Total hours worked by employees	(Enter amount)	(Enter amount)	(Enter amount)
Rate	Hourly rate for labor	(Enter amount)	(Enter amount)	(Enter amount)
Materials	Cost of materials used in production	(Enter amount)	(Enter amount)	(Enter amount)
Unit costs	Cost per unit of product	(Enter amount)	(Enter amount)	(Enter amount)
Total expenses	Sum of all budgeted expenses	(Enter amount)	(Enter amount)	(Enter amount)
Total revenue	Total income generated from sales	(Enter amount)	(Enter amount)	(Enter amount)
Profit/loss	Difference between total revenue and expenses	(Enter amount)	(Enter amount)	(Enter amount)

Summary

In this chapter, we've dove into the crucial aspects of securing funding for your entrepreneurial endeavors and mastering the fundamentals of money management. By now, you should feel equipped with a comprehensive understanding of various funding options and essential principles like budgeting, financial planning, and resource allocation. As I summarize our key takeaways, remember knowledge is power in the business world.

Looking ahead to the next chapter, I'll continue to build on this foundation by exploring essential business concepts, terminologies, and principles. Whether you're new to business or seeking to deepen your understanding, I will provide the tools to navigate key aspects vital for entrepreneurial success. Stay tuned as I shine a light on the legalities of forming a business as a teen, igniting curiosity and guiding you further on your entrepreneurial journey.

Chapter 7

The Basics of Business Structures

*Give your due diligence to understanding business
or you will have no place in it.*

—Daniel Lapin

T HESE WORDS ABOVE UNDERSCORE the fundamental truth that knowledge is the bedrock of success in
the business world. This chapter provides a solid foundation
in essential business concepts, terminology, and principles.
Whether you're a newcomer to the entrepreneurial landscape
or seeking to deepen your understanding, this will equip
you with the tools necessary to navigate the complexities of
business with confidence. From deciphering industry jargon
to grasping the intricacies of financial planning, the focus is
on empowering you to comprehend and apply key aspects
crucial for entrepreneurial success.

As we transcend the legalities of forming a business, particularly for aspiring teen entrepreneurs, I assist with illuminating
the pathways to transforming entrepreneurial dreams into
reality. Join me as we explore business fundamentals, setting
the stage for your journey toward entrepreneurial excellence.

Key Terms

Understanding basic business terms is essential for any entrepreneur to navigate the business world effectively. You don't need an advanced degree to grasp these concepts. This section simplifies these terms to ensure they're accessible to everyone. Here's a breakdown of some fundamental business terms every entrepreneur should know:

Accounting: Accounting involves systematically recording and reporting financial transactions within a business. It can be complex so hiring a professional may be beneficial.

Accounts receivable: This represents the money owed to your business by customers for goods or services. It provides insight into your business's outstanding payments.

Accounts payable: Accounts payable refers to the amount your business owes creditors for goods or services received.

Assets: Assets encompass your business's financial holdings, including current assets like cash and fixed assets like equipment.

Liabilities: Liabilities are the debts your business owes to others, categorized as current or long-term.

Revenue: Revenue is the income generated from business activities within a specific period, calculated by multiplying the unit cost of goods or services by the units sold.

Expenses: These are the costs incurred to operate your business, such as equipment, utilities, or inventory. Legitimate business expenses are often tax-deductible.

Owner's equity: Represented as a percentage, owner's equity denotes the owner's share of business assets.

Balance sheet: This financial document overviews a business's assets, liabilities, and owner's equity.

Net profit: Also known as the bottom line, net profit is the difference between total revenues and all expenses.

Net loss: If expenses exceed revenues, a net loss occurs, emphasizing the importance of controlling company costs.

Profit margin: This metric measures the profit retained relative to total sales, calculated by dividing profit by revenue.

Cash flow: Cash flow tracks the movement of money in and out of your business, ideally ensuring a higher income flow than outflow.

Return on investment (ROI): ROI indicates the gain or loss on a business investment relative to its cost.

B2B/B2C: Business-to-business (B2B) businesses supply goods or services to other companies, while business-to-consumer (B2C) businesses directly serve end users or consumers.

Business Structures Explained

Understanding different business structures is crucial for entrepreneurs as it impacts various aspects of their venture, including legal obligations, taxation, and liability. Here's an overview of the main forms of business structures, along with their pros and cons, to help you make an informed decision:

Sole proprietorship

- **Overview**: Simplest form with one individual managing operations.

- **Pros**: Easy and inexpensive to set up; minimal ongoing requirements.

- **Cons**: Owners are personally liable for debts and obligations.

Partnership

- **Overview**: Involves two or more owners sharing responsibilities.

- **Pros**: Little paperwork, special taxation arrangement.

- **Cons**: Partners are personally liable for debts, and potential for disagreements.

Corporation

- **Overview**: Separate legal entity from owners; complex setup.

- **Pros**: Ability to raise capital; limited personal liability.

- **Cons**: More requirements; expensive setup.

Limited Liability Company (LLC)

- **Overview**: Hybrid structure combining aspects of sole proprietorship and partnerships with corporations.

- **Pros**: Personal liability protection; fewer requirements.

- **Cons**: Moderate investment to setup; compliance with state laws.

Each structure offers unique advantages and drawbacks, so it's important to align your choice with your specific needs and goals. Whether you prioritize simplicity, liability protection, or scalability, understanding these structures will guide you toward the most suitable option for your entrepreneurial journey.

The most common Business Structures

For small businesses, especially those led by young entrepreneurs, two common business structures are sole proprietorships and LLCs. These structures are popular among small businesses due to their simplicity, flexibility, and liability protection. Choosing the right structure depends on factors like your goals, level of risk, and long-term plans for the business. Understanding the nuances of each structure will help you make an informed decision that aligns with your business needs and aspirations.

Keep in mind that a business structure is not set in stone. As your company grows, you can change your business structure to match your evolving needs. For example, you might begin as a sole proprietor, but later take on a partner, or change your company to an LLC or corporation.

Sole Proprietorship

A sole proprietorship represents the simplest form of business ownership, wherein a single individual manages all aspects of the business without any legal distinction between the owner and the business entity.

A sole proprietorship is an unregistered business entity where one individual, known as the proprietor, operates the business. Unlike other business structures, there's no legal separation between the owner and the business. This means the proprietor is personally liable for all business obligations, debts, and liabilities.

Establishing a sole proprietorship is straightforward. No formal legal steps are required. Simply conducting business operations makes you a sole proprietor. However, there are some considerations.

Depending on your location and business type, you may need to obtain licenses and permits to operate legally. You can find the requirements by checking your state, county, and city websites. Here you will find everything you need to operate legally in your area.

If your business operates under a name different from your own, you may need to register a DBA (doing business as) name. This is most commonly done at the state level and information will also be found on your state's website.

While not mandatory for sole proprietors without employees, obtaining an Employer Identification Number (EIN) may be necessary for tax purposes. You can apply for an EIN at:

https://www.irs.gov/businesses/small-businesses-self-emplo yed/apply-for-an-employer-identification-number-ein-onlin e

Advantages of sole proprietorship

- **Minimal paperwork and low costs**: It's simple and inexpensive to set up and maintain.

- **Simplified taxes**: Business profits are treated as personal income, simplifying tax filings.

- **Control**: The proprietor has full control over business operations and decision-making.

- **Flexibility**: Operating as a sole proprietor allows for quick decision-making and flexibility in business activities.

Disadvantages of Sole Proprietorship

- **Unlimited liability**: The proprietor is personally liable for all business debts and obligations.

- **Difficulty in raising capital**: Sole proprietors may find it challenging to raise funds since they can't sell stock or shares in the business.

- **Lack of continuity**: The business is tied to the proprietor's life, making continuity uncertain if the proprietor dies or becomes incapacitated.

Decision-making between sole proprietorships and other structures:

When deciding between a sole proprietorship, LLC, or corporation, consider your business's needs and objectives. A sole proprietorship is ideal for new entrepreneurs due to its simplicity and low cost. However, businesses requiring funding or facing potential liability risks may benefit from forming an LLC or corporation. Ultimately, understanding your business requirements and objectives will guide you in selecting the most suitable business structure.

Partnership

A partnership is a business structure formed by two or more parties who jointly own and operate the business. These parties, known as partners, can be individuals, corporations, or other legal entities. Partners contribute various resources like capital, labor, skills, and experience to the business:

There are two types of partnerships:

General Partnership (GP): In a general partnership, two or more partners jointly own and manage the business, sharing unlimited legal liability for the business's debts and obligations.

Limited Partnership (LP): A limited partnership consists of at least one general partner with unlimited liability and one or more limited partners who contribute capital but have limited liability.

If you're considering forming a business partnership, it's essential to understand the advantages and disadvantages of this business structure. Here's a breakdown:

Advantages of a partnership

- **Extra set of hands**: When you have a business partner, you're not navigating the entrepreneurial journey alone. Partners can help shoulder the workload, allowing tasks to be completed more efficiently.

- **Additional knowledge**: Partners bring diverse skills and expertise to the table, complementing each other's strengths. This collective knowledge can lead to more informed decision-making and innovative problem-solving.

- **Less financial burden**: Starting a business often requires a significant financial investment. With a partner, you can share the financial responsibilities, easing the burden on individual partners and potentially expanding the business's financial capacity.

- **Less paperwork**: Unlike some other business structures, forming a partnership involves minimal paperwork. While a partnership agreement outlining roles and responsibilities is necessary, the administrative requirements are generally straightforward.

- **Fewer tax forms**: Partnerships streamline tax obligations by passing through profits and losses to individual partners. This means no separate business entity taxes and simplified tax filings.

Disadvantages of a partnership

- **No solo decision-making**: In a partnership, decisions must be made collaboratively. This can slow the decision-making process and require consensus among partners, limiting individual autonomy.

- **Disagreements**: Conflict is inevitable in any collaborative venture. Partners may have differing opinions and goals, leading to disagreements that can impact business operations and relationships.

- **Shared profits**: While partnerships distribute profits among partners, this also means that individual partners must share the rewards of the business's success. Depending on the partnership agreement, this may result in smaller individual profit shares.

- **Not a separate legal entity**: A partnership does not provide legal separation between the business and its owners. Partners are personally liable for the business's debts and obligations, exposing personal assets to potential risks.

- **Individually taxed**: While pass-through taxation can be advantageous, it also means that partners are taxed individually at their respective tax rates. This may result in higher overall tax liabilities compared to other business structures.

Before committing to a partnership, consider these pros and cons carefully. Asking pertinent questions about compatibility, liability, and partnership type can help ensure partnership aligns with your business goals and preferences.

Steps to Establishing a Partnership

Forming a partnership is a straightforward process that begins with a mutual agreement between two or more individuals to enter into business together. While there's no need for formal paperwork to create a partnership, certain steps must be followed to ensure legal compliance and operational readiness. Here's a detailed overview:

1. **Choose a partnership name**: Partnerships can operate under the individual partners' last names or adopt a trade name, also known as a "DBA" (doing business as). Carefully select a name that's distinct and not already in use by another entity within your jurisdiction.

2. **Register your trade name (DBA)**: If opting for a

trade name, registration is typically required with the appropriate state or local authorities. This process involves submitting the necessary paperwork and potentially publishing a notice in a local newspaper to inform the public of your business name.

3. **Draft and sign a partnership agreement**: While not mandatory, a partnership agreement is highly recommended to outline each partner's roles, responsibilities, contributions, profit-sharing arrangements, decision-making processes, and procedures for dispute resolution. This document helps prevent misunderstandings and legal conflicts down the line.

4. **Comply with tax and regulatory requirements**: Partnerships must adhere to licensing, tax, and regulatory obligations applicable to all businesses. This includes obtaining an Employer Identification Number (EIN) from the IRS, securing any necessary business licenses, registering for state taxes, and fulfilling employer registration requirements if hiring employees.

5. **Obtain business insurance**: Given that partners are personally liable for the partnership's debts and obligations, securing adequate business insurance is essential for financial protection. General business liability insurance can safeguard against unforeseen liabilities and legal claims. Additionally, depending on

your industry and location, other forms of insurance, such as workers' compensation and commercial auto insurance, may be required.

By following these steps and seeking legal guidance when necessary, aspiring entrepreneurs can establish a partnership that complies with legal requirements, mitigates risks, and sets a solid foundation for business operations.

Steps to Establishing a Corporation

Considering the advantages of tax savings, investor appeal, personal protection, and enhanced credibility, forming a corporation might be the ideal move for your business. Here's a detailed breakdown of the incorporation process:

1. **Choose a business name**: Your first task in establishing a corporation is selecting a business name. Ensure it complies with state regulations by including a corporate identifier like "Inc." or "Co." Additionally, verify its availability and avoid restricted words by consulting your state's Secretary of State office.

2. **Register a DBA**: If you plan to operate under a different name than your corporate name, registering a "Doing Business As" (DBA) or fictitious name is necessary. Familiarize yourself with state guidelines and file accordingly with the Secretary of State's of-

fice.

3. **Appoint directors**: Owners typically appoint directors to oversee corporate governance. Directors' duties include managing business affairs, electing officers, and attending meetings. Adhere to state laws regarding the number and selection of directors.

4. **File articles of incorporation**: Complete and file articles of incorporation with the Secretary of State's office to formally establish your corporation as a separate legal entity. Include essential details such as the corporation's name, address, purpose, registered agent, and stock issuance specifics.

5. **Write corporate bylaws**: Develop corporate bylaws outlining governance procedures, stock issuance regulations, and meeting protocols. Although not mandatory for filing, bylaws are crucial for internal governance and legal compliance.

6. **Draft a shareholder agreement**: Consider crafting a shareholder agreement to safeguard shareholders' interests in various scenarios like ownership transfers or shareholder deaths. While optional, this agreement ensures clarity and fairness in unforeseen circumstances.

7. **Hold the initial board of directors meeting**: Convene an inaugural board meeting to adopt cor-

porate bylaws, appoint officers, authorize stock issuance, and discuss potential S corporation status
elections.

8. **Issue stock**: After obtaining board approval, issue
stock certificates to raise capital. Maintain meticulous records of stock transactions, including pur-
chaser details, share quantities, costs, and dates.

9. **Obtain business permits and licenses**: Secure all
necessary permits and licenses before commencing
business operations. Compliance requirements vary
based on location, industry, and business activities.

10. **Register your business**: Obtain tax identification
numbers from the IRS and state revenue agencies
to ensure proper tax reporting and compliance. Understand the taxation implications specific to your
corporation's type and jurisdiction.

11. **Open a corporate bank account**: Finally, establish a separate corporate bank account to segregate
business funds from personal assets. Consult with
your bank to gather the required documentation and
facilitate account setup.

Corporation Advantages and Drawbacks

Examining the advantages and drawbacks of a corporation can aid in determining the optimal business structure for your needs. Here's an exploration of the key pros and cons of a corporation:

Advantages of the corporation's business structure

- **Limited liability protection**: Shareholders enjoy limited liability, safeguarding their personal assets from business liabilities and lawsuits.

- **Tax benefits**: Corporations may benefit from tax deductions on various expenses, while owners can receive tax-free benefits like retirement plans and insurance.

- **Credibility**: Operating as a corporation can enhance the company's credibility and professionalism in the eyes of investors, customers, and partners.

- **Separate legal entity**: A corporation is a distinct legal entity, offering a clear separation between personal and corporate assets and liabilities.

- **Power structure**: Corporations have a defined power structure, with a board of directors overseeing operations, providing clarity and accountability.

- **Capital raising**: Publicly traded corporations can raise capital by selling shares and issuing bonds, offering a convenient avenue for funding expansion and growth.

Drawbacks of the corporation business structure

- **Complexity**: Establishing and operating a corporation entails more complexity and paperwork than other business structures, requiring meticulous adherence to regulations and formalities.

- **Cost**: The formation and maintenance of a corporation can be costlier than other business entities due to filing fees, legal expenses, and ongoing compliance requirements.

- **Double taxation for C Corps**: C Corporations face double taxation, with the entity paying taxes on profits and shareholders paying taxes on dividends, potentially reducing overall profitability.

- **Less control**: Shareholders have less direct control compared to other business structures because major decisions are made by the board of directors.

- **Corporate formalities**: Corporations must adhere to strict formalities, including holding annual meetings, maintaining records, and following bylaws, which can be time-consuming and burdensome.

Steps to Establishing an LLC

Entrepreneurs can successfully establish an LLC that suits their business needs and objectives by following these steps:

1. **Choose a state**: Select the state in which you want to form your LLC, considering factors like taxation, fees, and legal requirements.

2. **Choose a name & register it**: Select a unique name for your LLC and ensure it complies with state naming regulations. Conduct a name search and reserve the name if necessary.

3. **Choose a registered agent**: Appoint a registered agent with a physical address in the formation state to receive legal documents on behalf of the LLC.

4. **Prepare an LLC operating agreement**: Draft a comprehensive operating agreement outlining the rights, responsibilities, and management structure of the LLC, even if you're the sole member.

5. **File LLC articles of organization**: Submit the required formation documents, often called Articles of Organization or Certificate of Formation, to the Secretary of State's office.

6. **Obtain an EIN & bank account**: Apply for an Employer Identification Number (EIN) from the IRS, which serves as the LLC's tax ID, and open a business bank account using the EIN.

7. **Obtain business licenses and permits**: Research and obtain any necessary licenses and permits for your LLC's operations, complying with local, state, and federal regulations.

8. **Get tax advice and file any required forms**: Consult with a tax advisor to understand your LLC's tax obligations and file any necessary tax forms, ensuring compliance with tax laws.

Benefits of Forming an LLC

Understanding the advantages and drawbacks of forming a Limited Liability Company (LLC) can guide entrepreneurs in making informed decisions about their business structure. Let's examine the benefits and disadvantages of an LLC:

- **Limited liability**: LLC members are shielded from personal liability for the company's debts and obligations, protecting their private assets from business liabilities.

- **Flexible membership**: LLCs can have individual members, partnerships, trusts, or corporations, with no limit on the number of members, offering versatility in ownership structure.

- **Management structure**: Members can choose to manage the LLC themselves or appoint managers, providing flexibility in organizational management.

- **Pass-through taxation**: LLCs typically don't pay taxes at the entity level; instead, profits and losses are passed through to the member's personal tax returns, simplifying taxation.

- **Heightened credibility**: Operating as an LLC can enhance a business's credibility and professionalism, potentially attracting more clients, partners, and investors.

- **Limited compliance requirements**: Compared to corporations, LLCs face fewer state-imposed compliance obligations and ongoing formalities, reducing administrative burdens.

- **Transferable ownership**: Transferring ownership in an LLC is less complex than with corporations, often requiring unanimous approval from existing members, potentially limiting flexibility.

Drawbacks of Forming an LLC

- **Cost**: Establishing and maintaining an LLC can be more expensive than sole proprietorships or partnerships due to formation fees, annual report fees, and other state-imposed costs.

- **Compliance obligations**: While fewer than corporations, LLCs still have ongoing compliance requirements, such as annual filings and maintaining operating agreements, which can entail additional time and effort.

Legal Requirements for Teen Entrepreneurs

Creating a business as a teenager is a feasible and increasingly popular choice among young entrepreneurs. However, there are legal considerations to remember, along with variations in state regulations regarding minors owning businesses. Let's explore these aspects in detail:

Many states allow minors to establish businesses, while others specify an age requirement of 18 or older to form a business entity like an LLC. States such as Colorado, Illinois, Minnesota, and Oregon impose such restrictions. In states where minors are prohibited from forming businesses independently, alternative approaches include having a parent or guardian establish the company on their behalf or creating it in a different state with more lenient regulations.

States that allow minors to own businesses

Fortunately, most states permit minors to initiate businesses. For example, states like Texas, California, Delaware, Nevada, Wyoming, and Montana allow minors to establish LLCs and sole proprietorships. However, certain limitations may apply to teen entrepreneurs, such as restrictions on entering contracts or obtaining certain licenses, like those for liquor and tobacco.

Insurance Considerations

Teen entrepreneurs should also consider insurance for their businesses, although age restrictions may apply for obtaining certain types of insurance. It's advisable to consult with a qualified insurance broker to discuss suitable insurance options tailored to the business structure and operations. By understanding these legal requirements and insurance considerations, teenage entrepreneurs can navigate starting and operating a business effectively, setting themselves up for success in their entrepreneurial endeavors.

Businesses Taxes

Various types of taxes impose obligations on entrepreneurs and understanding them is crucial for compliance and financial planning. Let's explore the key types of taxes entrepreneurs should be aware of:

1. **Income tax**: Businesses must file income tax returns annually, with the structure of the business determining the applicable forms. All businesses, regardless of structure, are subject to income tax obligations.

2. **Estimated income tax**: Unlike employees who have taxes withheld from their paychecks, businesses typically make quarterly payments based on their anticipated income tax for the year. Individual taxpayers use Form 1040-ES, while corporations use Form 1120-W for estimation purposes.

3. **Self-employment tax**: Individuals working for themselves are responsible for self-employment tax, which contributes to Social Security and Medicare. This tax applies if earnings exceed $400 annually or wages surpass $108.28 from tax-exempt entities like churches or religious organizations.

4. **Employment taxes**: Entrepreneurs with employees must handle employment taxes, including Social Se-

curity, Medicare, the federal income tax, and the federal unemployment tax. Employers are responsible for filing and paying these taxes on behalf of their employees.

5. **Federal excise tax**: Certain businesses are subject to federal excise taxes, which apply to specific products, activities, or equipment. While most small businesses may not encounter these taxes, compliance is essential for those in relevant industries.

Common Tax Deductions for Entrepreneurs

Tax laws have evolved to provide relief for the additional expenses of self-employed individuals. The Tax Cuts and Jobs Act (TCJA), enacted during the Trump administration, introduced significant changes to tax deductions for self-employed taxpayers, some of which are temporary and slated to expire in 2025. One notable change brought about by the TCJA is the introduction of the qualified business income (QBI) deduction for pass-through businesses. This deduction offers a substantial benefit to owners of sole proprietorships, partnerships, S corporations, and certain LLCs. Eligible taxpayers can deduct up to 20% of their QBI, providing a significant tax advantage. The QBI deduction is calculated based on the net amount of qualified items of income, gain, deduction, and loss from a qualified trade or business. This deduction is a valuable tax-saving tool for self-employed individuals, allowing them to reduce their taxable income effectively. However, it's essential to review deductions annually to optimize business profitability. Common deductions available to self-employed individuals include:

Self-employment tax deduction

- Self-employed individuals are responsible for paying Medicare and Social Security taxes, which constitute the self-employment tax.

- The self-employment tax rate is 15.3%, with 12.4% allocated to Social Security and 2.9% to Medicare.

- Self-employed individuals can deduct half of the self-employment tax from their net income when calculating income tax, reducing their overall tax liability.

Home office deduction

- Self-employed individuals can deduct expenses related to a home office used exclusively and regularly for business purposes.

- Eligible expenses include the business percentage of rent, mortgage interest, utilities, insurance, and repairs.

Internet and phone bill deduction

- Business-related phone and internet expenses can be

deducted, provided they are directly related to the business.

- Only expenses directly attributable to business use are deductible.

Health insurance premium deduction

- Self-employed individuals can deduct health insurance premiums paid for themselves, their spouses, dependents, and children under 27.

- The deduction applies to health, dental, and qualified long-term care insurance premiums.

Meals deduction

- Meal expenses incurred during business travel, client entertainment, or business conferences are deductible.

- The deduction is typically limited to 50% of the meal's actual cost, or the standard meal allowance.

Travel deduction

- Business-related travel expenses, including transportation, lodging, and meals, are deductible if they meet certain criteria.

- Travel must have a specific business purpose and take place away from the individual's tax home.

Vehicle use deduction

- Expenses associated with using a vehicle for business purposes, such as mileage, gas, and maintenance, are deductible.

- Self-employed individuals can choose between the standard mileage rate and the actual expense method for calculating deductions.

Interest deduction

- Interest on business loans is tax-deductible, including interest on credit cards used for business expenses.

Dues and publications deduction

- Expenses for professional memberships, subscriptions to business-related publications, and specialized books are deductible.

Retirement plan contributions deduction

- Contributions to retirement plans, such as SEP-IRAs, SIMPLE IRAs, and solo 401(k)s, are deductible, providing tax savings and retirement benefits.

Understanding and maximizing available deductions can significantly reduce tax liabilities for self-employed individuals, contributing to overall business profitability and financial success.

How to File Your Taxes

Here's a breakdown of the steps to file your small business taxes:

1. **Collect your tax records**: Assemble all the necessary documents for tax filing, including invoices, bills, receipts, and financial statements.

2. **Identify required IRS forms**: Determine which IRS forms apply to your business structure, such as Schedule C for sole proprietors or Form 1065 for partnerships.

3. **Complete tax forms**: Fill out the required tax forms accurately, ensuring you provide all necessary information. If using software, follow the prompts carefully.

4. **Be aware of tax deadlines**: Know the deadlines for filing small business taxes, which vary depending on your business structure and fiscal year-end.

5. **Consider a tax extension**: If you need more time to file your taxes, consider applying for a business tax extension using Form 7004. This grants a six-month extension, though it doesn't extend the time to pay

taxes.

6. **Submit your tax return**: File your small business taxes before the deadline, either electronically or by mail. Ensure compliance with tax laws and make any necessary tax payments.

7. **Manage tax payments**: Stay on top of your tax payments throughout the year by making estimated tax payments as required. This helps avoid penalties and prepares you for the end-of-year tax bill.

Remember, maximizing your deductions reduces your taxable income and lowers your tax bill. Keep detailed records of all business expenses and consult a tax professional as needed.

Saving money on taxes

Here are some strategies to reduce your tax burden as an entrepreneur:

Leverage business deductions:

Take advantage of allowable business expenses to lower your taxable income. Properly document cash expenses and ensure compliance with tax regulations to maximize deductions.

Invest in energy-efficient equipment:

Investing in energy-efficient equipment and systems not only benefits the environment but also qualifies for tax credits or deductions, reducing your tax liability.

Utilize tax-advantaged retirement accounts:

Consider contributing to tax-advantaged retirement accounts such as IRAs or 401(k)s to lower your taxable income and save for retirement.

Prioritize paying yourself:

Pay yourself a reasonable salary from your business profits, which can be taxed at a lower rate than other forms of income.

Explore selling appreciated assets:

Selling appreciated assets strategically can help you take advantage of favorable tax treatment, such as capital gains tax rates, potentially reducing your overall tax liability.

Implementing these tax-saving strategies keeps more of your hard-earned money and optimizes your financial situation as an entrepreneur.

Navigating Legal Contracts

Here's a guide for entrepreneurs on navigating legal contracts and agreements for common start-ups:

Partnership agreements:

These agreements outline the rights and responsibilities of business co-founders, including ownership stakes, decision-making authority, and capital contributions.

Shareholder agreements:

Governing relations between shareholders in a corporation, these agreements cover stock ownership, transfer restrictions, dividend policies, and voting arrangements.

Operating agreements:

For LLCs, these agreements define ownership percentages, roles and responsibilities, capital contributions, and decision-making processes.

Investment agreements:

These contracts detail terms for investment rounds, including investment amounts, securities issued, investor rights, and exit strategies.

Convertible note agreements:

This relates to short-term debt that converts into equity shares. These agreements include terms such as loan amount, interest rate, conversion discount, and valuation cap.

Loan agreements:

Necessary for bank financing, these agreements specify the loan amount, interest rate, repayment terms, collateral, loan covenants, and personal guarantees.

Intellectual property agreements:

This covers licensing, royalties, confidentiality, and intellectual property like patents, trademarks, and copyrights.

Key Contract Negotiation Tips for Entrepreneurs

- **Take time for due diligence**: Carefully review contracts and research unfamiliar terms before signing.

- **Hire legal counsel**: Have a lawyer experienced with start-ups review substantial agreements whenever possible.

- **Clarify ambiguous language**: Flag vague clauses and push for specific, measurable terms to avoid misunderstandings.

- **Outline major deal breakers**: Identify fundamental provisions you won't compromise on to protect your interests.

- **Add exit strategies**: Include realistic termination provisions in long-term contracts to mitigate risks.

Effectively manage your legal obligations and protect your interests by understanding these contracts and negotiation tips.

Summary

In this chapter, I've laid down the cornerstone of your journey into the business world, equipping you with fundamental concepts, terminology, and principles essential for entrepreneurial success. From understanding common start-up contracts to navigating legalities as a teen entrepreneur, you've gained insights critical for building a solid foundation.

As you transition to the next phase of your entrepreneurial journey, get ready to dive into the exciting realm of advertising, branding, and marketing. In the upcoming chapter, you'll master the art of strategically promoting your business and crafting a compelling brand presence. We'll explore the importance of building an online presence and provide you with actionable strategies to make your mark in the digital landscape. So, get ready to elevate your business to new heights as we submerge into the world of marketing and branding, empowering you to stand out in the competitive marketplace and capture the attention of your target audience. Get ready to unleash your creativity and strategic prowess as I pave the way for your entrepreneurial success!

Chapter 8
Brand Building and Online Presence

Let excellence be your brand... when you are ex-
cellent, you become unforgettable.
                                        –Oprah Winfrey

I N THE COMPETITIVE WORLD of entrepreneurship, these words above resonate deeply. Excellence is not just a goal; it is a standard that defines your brand and makes it memorable. This chapter guides you through mastering the essentials of advertising, branding, and marketing, all key components of strategically promoting your business and establishing a compelling brand presence.

We'll explore the core principles of advertising, from crafting impactful messages to choosing the right channels to reach your audience. You'll learn the art of branding and understanding how to create a unique identity that reflects your values and resonates with your customers.

Marketing strategies will be dissected, providing you with tools to engage your target market and drive business growth. We'll also examine the significance of building an online presence in today's digital age. You'll discover practical tips on creating and maintaining a strong online footprint, leveraging social media, websites, and other digital platforms to enhance visibility and connect with your audience.

By the end of this chapter, you'll be equipped with the knowledge and strategies to elevate your business through excellence in advertising, branding, and marketing, ensuring your brand becomes unforgettable in the minds of your customers.

Building an Online Presence

Why is it Important?

In today's digital age, having a robust online presence is crucial for businesses. Let's explore the significant benefits that come with establishing your brand online:

Increased trust:

A strong online presence helps build trust with potential customers. When people see that your business is active and engaged online, they are more likely to view it as credible and reliable. This trust can drive sales and attract new customers. Online reviews and testimonials can further enhance this trust by providing social proof of your business's quality and reliability.

Increased visibility:

Visibility is key to business success. It exposes your business to a broader audience. Platforms like Google My Business can significantly boost your local visibility, making it easier for nearby customers to discover and engage with your company.

Additionally, an online presence allows you to reach customers worldwide, expanding your market far beyond your physical location.

Increased brand awareness:

Brand awareness is vital for long-term success. An online presence enables you to consistently communicate your brand message across various platforms, making your business more recognizable to potential customers. Regularly sharing valuable content and engaging with your audience helps solidify your brand identity and keeps it top-of-mind.

Key Elements of Building an Online Presence

Here's a brief overview of the essential elements involved in establishing a strong online presence, as discussed in detail in the preceding chapter on marketing:

Website design and development

- **Foundation**: Your website is the cornerstone of your online presence. It should be professional, user-friendly, and optimized for search engines to attract and retain visitors.

- **Branding**: Incorporate your branding strategy into your website design, including mission and vision statements, business name, and logo, to ensure consistency and professionalism.

Search Engine Optimization (SEO)

- **Visibility**: SEO is crucial for making your website visible in search engine results. Optimizing your website with relevant keywords improves your search rankings and attracts more organic traffic.

- **Content optimization**: Optimize all content on your website, including images, text, and web pages, to enhance your site's efficiency and discoverability.

Social media marketing

- **Engagement**: Social media platforms are vital for reaching and engaging with your audience. Choose platforms relevant to your target audience, and post engaging content regularly.

- **Community Management**: Implement effective community management to respond to queries promptly and maintain active engagement with your followers.

Blog posting

- **Content**: Use blogs to provide valuable information to your audience. This can include product information, industry insights, how-to guides, and case studies.

- **Engagement**: Regular blog posts keep your audience informed and engaged, helping to establish your business as an authority in your industry.

Web analytics

- **Tracking**: Use web analytics tools like Google Analytics to monitor and analyze your website's performance. This data helps you understand your audience's behavior and refine your content strategy accordingly.

- **Optimization**: Adjust your strategies based on analytics to improve visitor engagement and conversion rates.

Focusing on these key elements allows you to build a robust online presence that enhances visibility, builds trust, and increases brand awareness. This foundation helps you reach more customers, create lasting relationships, and drive business growth.

Building Your Brand Identity

A brand identity encompasses the visible and intangible elements that create a company's distinct persona. Key components include the logo, design, voice, values, mission, and the overall perception customers and employees have of the company. These elements work synergistically to project a cohesive and recognizable image.

Why is brand identity important?

A strong brand identity is crucial because it creates recognition and builds trust. It is a visual and emotional representation of the company, making it memorable. Consistency in brand identity fosters trust and credibility among customers and stakeholders.

Your brand identity guides marketing efforts. It offers a consistent template for all marketing and communication efforts, ensuring alignment with the company's mission and values. This helps attract and retain customers. A strong identity draws in new customers and maintains loyalty among existing ones.

A strong brand identity also enhances talent acquisition. A reputable brand attracts quality job candidates, enhancing the overall recruitment experience. People want to work for brands they know and identify with.

Building a Strong Brand Identity

Research your competition:

Analyze competitors to understand their branding strategies. Identify their strengths and weaknesses to inform your own approach.

Understand your target audience:

Develop detailed customer personas to grasp what your audience desires and expects from your brand.

Define your brand personality:

Determine the traits and characteristics that best represent your brand. This personality should align with your company's values and appeal to your target audience.

Create a unique look and feel:

Develop a distinctive visual identity, including a logo, color palette, typography, and overall design style that sets your brand apart.

Develop a consistent brand voice and tone:

Establish guidelines for the language and tone used in all communications. Consistency in voice ensures a uniform experience across all customer interactions.

Involve your audience in your brand:

Engage your audience through interactive content and solicit feedback to foster a sense of community and loyalty.

Evaluate and adapt:

Regularly assess your brand's performance and make necessary adjustments. Stay responsive to market trends and customer feedback to keep your brand relevant.

Creating a Unique Brand Identity

To create a unique brand identity, follow these steps:

1. **Establish clear goals and strategy**: Define what you want to achieve with your brand identity. Consider your company's mission, values, and long-term goals.

2. **Align with core values and mission**: Ensure every branding decision reflects your company's core values and mission to build a trustworthy reputation.

3. **Assess Current perception**: Conduct surveys and gather feedback from customers and employees to understand how your brand is currently perceived.

4. **Know your audience**: Use customer personas to tailor your brand identity to meet the expectations and preferences of your target audience.

5. **Research competitors**: Analyze your competitors to identify opportunities for differentiation.

6. **Create visual and verbal elements**: Design a logo, choose colors, select fonts, and develop a brand voice that together creates a cohesive and unique brand identity.

7. **Implement and monitor**: Roll out your new brand

identity across all platforms and continuously monitor its performance, adjusting as needed to stay relevant and effective.

Following these steps guides the development of a strong and unique brand identity that resonates with your audience, stands out in the market, and supports your business goals.

Unique Brand Identity Examples

- **Peter McKinnon**, a photographer and filmmaker, has built a brand identity around authentic creativity. His personal style and engaging content make his brand easily recognizable and relatable.

- **Quiksilver** has established itself as a leading brand in the surfing community. Its identity is deeply rooted in the surfing lifestyle, as reflected in its products, marketing, and brand ethos.

- **National Geographic's** brand identity revolves around exploration and discovery. It consistently communicates a sense of adventure and curiosity through compelling storytelling and breathtaking visuals,

Brand Archetypes

What is a brand archetype?

A brand archetype is a framework that embodies a set of fundamental human values, allowing brands to develop a distinctive and engaging identity. This concept, rooted in Carl Jung's personality archetypes from 1919, helps brands connect emotionally with their audience by personifying certain traits and narratives.

Why is it important to identify your brand archetype?

Identifying your brand archetype is crucial because it offers several key benefits. It not only establishes a consistent brand identity but also increases brand awareness and brand loyalty.

A clear brand archetype differentiates your brand in a crowded market, making it more memorable. People are more likely to remember and connect with stories and characters, which enhances brand recognition.

A defined archetype ensures consistent messaging across all platforms, reinforcing your brand's identity and making it easily recognizable. Resonating with your audience's emotions and values, a strong brand archetype fosters deeper connections, encouraging customer loyalty and repeat business.

The 12 Brand Archetypes

1. The Outlaw

- **Key features**: Rebellious, disruptive, independent.

- **Pros**: Strong, loyal following; stands out in the market.

- **Cons**: Can alienate more conservative audiences.

- **Examples**: Harley-Davidson, Virgin Group, Diesel.

2. The Creator

- **Key features**: Innovative, artistic, imaginative.

- **Pros**: Appeals to creatives; promotes innovation.

- **Cons**: Can be seen as impractical or niche.

- **Examples**: Adobe, Lego, Crayola.

3. The Magician

- **Key features**: Visionary, charismatic, transformative.

- **Pros**: Inspires wonder and loyalty; drives innovation.

- Cons: High expectations can lead to disappointment.

- Examples: Apple, Disney, Nintendo.

4. The Hero

- Key features: Courageous, determined, influential.

- Pros: Inspires action; builds a strong, positive image.

- Cons: Can seem overly intense or aggressive.

- Examples: Nike, Duracell, FedEx.

5. The Lover

- Key features: Passionate, indulgent, empathetic.

- Pros: Creates strong emotional connections; appeals to desires.

- Cons: Can seem superficial or exclusive.

- Examples: Victoria's Secret, Chanel, Tiffany & Co.

6. The Jester

- Key features: Fun, light-hearted, spontaneous.

- **Pros**: Highly engaging; memorable.

- **Cons**: Risk of not being taken seriously.

- **Examples**: Wendy's, Ben & Jerry's, Old Spice.

7. The Everyman

- **Key features**: Relatable, humble, friendly.

- **Pros**: Broad appeal; fosters loyalty.

- **Cons**: Can lack distinctiveness.

- **Examples**: Levi's, Gap, IKEA.

8. The Caregiver

- **Key features**: Compassionate, nurturing, supportive.

- **Pros**: Builds trust and strong emotional bonds.

- **Cons**: Can be perceived as dull or overly serious.

- **Examples**: Johnson & Johnson, Allstate Insurance, Campbell's Soup.

9. The Ruler

- **Key features**: Authoritative, responsible, organized.

- Pros: Conveys reliability and quality; commands respect.

- Cons: Can seem controlling or elitist.

- Examples: Rolex, Louis Vuitton, IBM.

10. **The Innocent**

- **Key features**: Optimistic, honest, pure.

- **Pros**: Builds trust and positive associations.

- **Cons**: Can seem naïve or simplistic.

- **Examples**: Coca-Cola, Dove.

11. **The Sage**

- **Key features**: Wise, knowledgeable, articulate.

- **Pros**: Establishes authority; trusted source of information.

- **Cons**: Can seem dry or overly intellectual.

- **Examples**: Google, BBC, National Geographic.

12. **The Explorer**

- **Key features**: Adventurous, ambitious, independent.

- ○ **Pros**: Inspires innovation; appeals to adventurous spirits.

- ○ **Cons**: Can seem restless or non-conformist.

- ○ **Examples**: The North Face, Jeep, GoPro.

How to Choose Your Brand Archetype

Choosing the right brand archetype involves several steps:

Identify your brand's mission and values:

Start by defining what your brand stands for and its core values. For instance, a brand focused on innovation might align with the Creator archetype, while one prioritizing care and support might fit the Caregiver archetype.

Understand your target audience:

Conduct thorough market research to understand your audience's needs, desires, and values. This will help you select an archetype that resonates with them.

Build on emotion:

Determine the emotional response you want to evoke in your audience. For example, an Explorer archetype should evoke feelings of freedom and adventure.

Ensure consistency across all touchpoints:

Maintain consistency in your branding elements, including logos, color schemes, taglines, and marketing efforts. This cohesive approach ensures a unified brand experience, making your brand more memorable.

Carefully selecting and consistently applying a brand archetype creates a compelling and relatable brand identity that fosters connections with your audience and stands out in the marketplace.

What Leads to Brand Distrust?

In the digital age, consumer trust in brands is intricately tied to how companies handle personal data. As consumers spend more time online, transparency and ethical data practices become paramount. Here are the top reasons why consumers may lose trust in a brand:

Misuse of personal data:

Consumers today are highly sensitive about how their personal data is used. When brands send emails or make offers based on data consumers did not knowingly share, trust erodes. This lack of transparency can make consumers feel like their privacy is being invaded.

Over-collection of personal information:

Asking for too much personal information is a major red flag for consumers. According to a report by Jebbit, 35% of consumers cited excessive data requests as the top reason for losing trust in a brand. This indicates the importance of limiting data collection to only what is necessary and being clear about why it is needed.

Data scandals:

Public data breaches or scandals significantly damage consumer trust. Approximately 21.1% of consumers mentioned that data scandals lead to distrust. Brands must prioritize robust data security measures to prevent such incidents and maintain consumer confidence.

Intrusive advertising:

Advertisements that feel overly targeted or "creepy" can make consumers uncomfortable. This type of advertising was identified as a reason for distrust by 18.2% of respondents. Brands should aim for a balance between personalization and privacy, ensuring ads are relevant but not intrusive.

Complicated privacy policies:

Confusing or opaque privacy policies contribute to consumer distrust. Clear, straightforward communication about how data is used and protected builds trust. Brands should avoid legal jargon and make privacy policies easily understandable.

Lack of value from data use:

Consumers are more likely to trust brands that provide clear benefits from the data they collect. Nearly 32% of respondents indicated improved experiences based on their data increased trust. Brands should focus on delivering tangible value through personalized recommendations and services.

Lack of interactive and personalized experiences:

Interactive experiences, like product matches and personality quizzes, significantly enhance trust. These activities provide transparency and immediate value, leading to a 38.4% increase in consumer trust. Personalized emails, based on willingly shared data, also contribute positively to trust.

Make Your Brand More Credible

Establishing and enhancing your brand's credibility is essential for attracting and retaining customers. Credibility encompasses the trust and authority your brand holds in the eyes of your audience. A credible brand appears more reliable and commands higher respect and customer loyalty. Here's a closer look at what credibility means, why it's important, and practical tips to build it.

What is credibility?

Credibility refers to the perception that your brand is trustworthy, reliable, and an expert in its field. It's built through consistent, ethical behavior, expertise, and delivering on promises. When a brand is credible, customers feel confident they will receive value and quality from it.

Can credibility attract more customers?

Absolutely. Credible brands are more likely to attract and retain customers. Customers who trust a brand, are more inclined to choose its products or services over competitors, even if those alternatives are cheaper. Credibility can lead to increased customer loyalty and higher conversion rates. Trustworthy brands build strong, long-term relationships with their customers. Potential customers are more likely to convert when they perceive a brand as credible. Credible brands benefit from positive recommendations.

Word-of-mouth referrals are a magical marketing tool that costs zero dollars.

Tips to Build a Credible Brand

Act professionally at all times:

Always conduct yourself and your business with professionalism. This means being punctual, respectful, and dependable. Consistent professional behavior builds a reputation for reliability and respectability.

Create social proof:

Social proof is critical to establishing credibility. This includes customer testimonials, case studies, awards, and endorsements. Displaying logos of reputable clients on your website, sharing positive reviews, and highlighting success stories can significantly enhance your brand's trustworthiness.

Become an expert in a niche:

Specialize in a specific area within your industry. Focus on a niche, develop deep expertise, and become the go-to authority. This specialization differentiates your brand and makes it more credible to those seeking expert knowledge.

Be an influencer:

Take an active role in your industry by leading discussions, sharing insights, and connecting people. Influencers shape industry trends and opinions, thereby building credibility.

Engage in activities like writing blogs, hosting events, and sharing valuable content on social media.

Get interviewed:

Seek interview opportunities with industry bloggers, podcasts, and media outlets. Being featured in interviews showcases your expertise and positions you as a thought leader, boosting your credibility among a broader audience.

Encourage referrals:

Satisfied customers are your best advocates. Ask them to refer your brand to others. A referral from a trusted source carries significant weight and enhances your brand's credibility through word-of-mouth marketing.

Be omnipresent:

Maintain a strong and consistent presence across multiple platforms. Engage in regular blogging, tweeting, networking, and other activities that keep your brand visible. Being omnipresent ensures that your brand stays top-of-mind and appears more reliable and accessible.

By integrating these strategies, you can significantly enhance your brand's credibility, attract higher-quality clients, and establish a stronger, more respected presence in your industry.

Brand Consistency

Maintaining brand consistency is crucial for creating a unified and recognizable identity that resonates with customers. Here's an in-depth look at what brand consistency entails, its benefits, the key elements involved, how to overcome challenges, and examples of brands that excel in this area.

What is brand consistency?

Brand consistency involves uniformly presenting your company across all marketing channels. This ensures your brand's image, messaging, and values are coherent and recognizable, whether customers encounter you online, in-store, or through advertising.

Benefits of brand consistency

Build customer trust:

Consistent branding fosters trust, as customers know what to expect from your brand. Trust is the foundation of customer loyalty and long-term relationships.

Recognition and recall:

A consistent brand makes it easier for customers to recognize and remember your brand. This significantly impacts their purchasing decisions and brand loyalty.

Emotional connection:

Consistent messaging and visuals help build an emotional connection with your audience. This connection is crucial for customer loyalty and advocacy.

Competitive advantage:

Standing out in a crowded market is easier when your brand maintains a consistent identity. It differentiates you from competitors and reinforces your unique value proposition.

Reduced confusion:

Clear and consistent branding reduces customer confusion. It ensures customers understand who you are, what you offer, and what you stand for, leading to a better overall customer experience.

Elements of Brand Consistency

- **Visual identity**: This includes your logo, color palette, typography, and imagery. Keeping these elements uniform across all platforms helps create a cohesive and recognizable brand.

- **Tone and messaging**: Your brand's voice and tone should be consistent in all communications. Maintaining a consistent tone builds familiarity and trust, whether it's a social media post, a customer service interaction, or a marketing email.

- **Customer experience**: Ensuring the customer experience is consistent across all touchpoints—from your website to your physical store—helps reinforce your brand's reliability and quality.

- **Adoption across all platforms**: Your brand's identity should be uniformly adopted across all platforms and channels. This includes social media, websites, advertising, packaging, and in-store experiences.

Overcoming Brand Consistency Challenges

Expanding branding across multiple platforms:

It can be challenging to maintain consistency across numerous platforms. Use brand guidelines and digital asset management tools to ensure all elements align with your brand identity.

Employee involvement:

Make certain all employees understand and embody the brand's values and messaging. Training and internal communication are key to maintaining brand consistency.

Evolving market trends:

Adapt to market trends without compromising your brand's core identity. Update your brand guidelines regularly to reflect changes while maintaining consistency.

Scaling up:

As your brand grows, maintaining consistency can become more complex. Implement robust brand management systems and processes to keep your brand consistent as you scale.

International markets and cultural differences:

Adapting your brand to different cultural contexts while maintaining consistency can be challenging. Research and understand local preferences and modify your branding appropriately without losing the core identity.

Brand Consistency Examples

1. **Nike**: Nike maintains a consistent brand through its iconic "swoosh" logo and "Just Do It" slogan. Their marketing, product design, and customer experience are aligned with their brand identity, reinforcing their position as a leader in the sportswear industry.

2. **Starbucks**: Starbucks uses a consistent color scheme, store layout, and customer service approach. Their brand identity is reflected in every aspect of their business, from the ambiance of their stores to the quality of their coffee, creating a recognizable and reliable experience.

3. **Mailchimp**: Mailchimp ensures brand consistency

through its playful and approachable tone, distinctive visual style, and comprehensive marketing tools. Their unified brand experience across digital platforms makes them a trusted choice for email marketing and automation.

Establishing and maintaining brand consistency helps build a strong, recognizable brand that stands out in the marketplace, fosters customer loyalty, and drives business growth.

Positioning Matters

The Role of Positioning in Branding

Brand positioning is critical in shaping how your audience perceives your brand relative to competitors. It defines a space in the minds of consumers, carving out a unique identity that differentiates your brand. This strategic approach is essential for businesses aiming to dominate their market:

What is brand positioning?

Brand positioning is the deliberate process of creating a distinctive image and identity for your brand in the minds of your target customers. It goes beyond a catchy tagline or an appealing logo; it's about crafting a unique place for your brand that resonates with your audience, making it stand out from the competition.

Key Elements of a Brand Positioning Statement

- **Target audience**: Clearly define who your ideal customers are. Understanding their needs, preferences, and behaviors is crucial.

- **Category or Industry**: Specify the market segment or industry in which your brand operates. This helps in identifying the competitive landscape.

- **Key differentiator**: Highlight what sets your brand apart from others. This could be a unique feature, superior quality, or exceptional service.

- **Value proposition**: Articulate the primary benefit your brand offers to customers. This is a compelling reason why customers should choose your brand over others.

Why Is Brand Positioning So Important?

Brand positioning is vital because it **distinguishes** your brand from competitors. Making it easily recognizable enhances brand awareness. Effective positioning keeps your brand in the minds of consumers.

Positioning your company communicates value by clearly conveying the unique benefits your brand offers. This justifies premium pricing by emphasizing quality or exclusivity. A well-positioned brand also controls its reputation, fostering trust and loyalty among customers.

Types of Brand Positioning Strategies

Customer service positioning strategy: Focuses on exceptional customer service to stand out. Brands like Apple use this strategy to justify higher prices and build loyalty through excellent support.

Convenience-based positioning strategy: Emphasizes the ease of use, accessibility, and time-saving benefits of a product. For example, Swiffer's products are marketed for convenience compared to traditional cleaning tools.

Price-based positioning strategy: Positions the brand as the most affordable option in the market. This strategy attracts cost-conscious consumers but may risk perceptions of lower quality.

Quality-based positioning strategy: Highlights superior quality, craftsmanship, and materials. Brands using this strategy, like Ferrari, appeal to consumers willing to pay a premium for exceptional products.

Differentiation strategy: Focuses on unique or innovative features that set the brand apart. Tesla is a prime example, offering cutting-edge technology in the electric vehicle market.

Social media positioning strategy: Utilizes social media channels to tell the brand's story and engage with customers.

This strategy involves choosing the right platforms where your target audience is most active and creating compelling content that resonates with them.

Creating a Brand Positioning Strategy

Determine your current brand positioning. Start by assessing how your brand is currently perceived in the market. Are you viewed as just another option, or do you stand out? To do this, analyze your target audience, your brand's mission, values, unique features, and overall persona. This self-assessment provides a foundation for the next steps.

Create a brand essence chart: Develop a brand essence chart to encapsulate what your brand represents to customers. This chart should include:

- **Attributes**: Key features of your product or service.

- **Benefits**: The customer experiences these attributes provide.

- **Personality**: Adjectives that describe your brand's character.

- **Source of authority**: Your brand's credibility and expertise.

- **Customer identity**: What your brand says about its customers.

- **Customer feelings**: Emotional responses your brand elicits.

- **Brand essence**: A concise statement summarizing the core of your brand.

Identify your competitors: Understanding who your competitors are is crucial. Use market research, customer feedback, and social media platforms to identify them. This knowledge will help you understand the competitive landscape and pinpoint opportunities for differentiation.

Conduct competitor research: Analyze your competitors' strengths, weaknesses, products, marketing strategies, and market positions. This research will help you identify gaps and opportunities where your brand can excel. Be objective to avoid internal biases.

Identify your unique value proposition: After evaluating your competitors, identify what makes your brand unique. This could be a particular strength your competitors lack. Highlight these unique aspects to form the basis of your positioning.

Build a brand positioning framework: Organize your insights into a comprehensive framework that includes:

- **Big idea**: The core concept driving your brand

- **Value proposition**: This is what makes your brand valuable to customers.

- **Target audience**: The specific group you aim to serve

- **Mission statement**: Your brand's purpose and goals

- **Tone of voice**: The style and attitude of your brand's communication

- **Elevator pitch**: A brief, compelling summary of your brand

- **Message pillars**: Key themes and messages

- **Sample touchpoints**: Practical applications in marketing materials

Create your positioning statement: Develop a concise statement that encapsulates your brand's unique offer and how it meets customer needs. Focus on the primary benefits and why your product or service is necessary.

Evaluate your positioning: Test and refine your positioning statement by gathering feedback from your target audience. Ensure it resonates and achieves its intended impact.

Establish an emotional connection: Build trust and a positive experience by connecting emotionally with prospects. Understand their needs and aspirations to create meaningful interactions.

Reinforce differentiating qualities during sales: Throughout the sales process consistently highlight what sets your brand apart. Use insights from your competitor analysis to emphasize your unique strengths.

Create value: Ensure your product or service genuinely solves a problem or fulfills a need. This will strengthen your brand's relevance and appeal.

Ensure customer-facing employees embody your brand: Train employees to represent your brand's core values and voice. Consistency in customer interactions reinforces your brand's authenticity and reliability.

Examples of Top Positioning Strategies

1. **Bumble vs. Tinder**: Bumble empowers women by allowing them to make the first move, contrasting Tinder's focus on casual connections. Bumble also expands beyond dating to friendships and professional networking, while Tinder remains primarily a dating app.

2. **Starbucks vs. Dunkin'**: Starbucks emphasizes a premium, in-store experience focused on quality, while Dunkin' promotes convenience and affordability with its coffee and donuts.

3. **Spotify vs. Apple Music**: Spotify leverages high personalization and a free plan, making it accessible,

M. A. GALLANT

whereas Apple Music focuses on a premium experience and a vast song library, appealing to Apple brand loyalists.

4. **Popeyes vs. Chick-fil-A**: Popeyes offers bold, southern flavors and positions itself as a down-home, reliable option available every day, while Chick-fil-A emphasizes consistent quality and exceptional customer service, despite being closed on Sundays.

5. **Target vs. Walmart**: Target aims to offer a higher-end experience with organized stores and quality service. Walmart focuses on low prices and wide accessibility, making it the go-to for convenience and affordability.

6. **Cash App vs. Venmo**: Cash App prioritizes speed and ease of transactions, while Venmo emphasizes social connections, making transactions feel more like a social activity.

7. **Peloton vs. Bowflex VeloCore**: Peloton appeals to younger, trend-conscious consumers with high social engagement, while Bowflex VeloCore offers a comparable product at a more accessible price point, emphasizing value.

8. **Google Meet vs. Zoom**: Zoom became synonymous with remote work during the pandemic, focusing on professional meetings while Google Meet

positioned itself as a versatile tool for both professional and personal connections.

Brand Voice

Brand voice is essentially the unique personality a brand cultivates to communicate with its target audience across various platforms. It encompasses the tone, style, and messaging consistency used to establish brand recognition and foster a deeper connection with consumers.

Differentiating between a brand's voice and tone is crucial. While brand voice represents the overall personality and character of the brand, tone refers to how that personality is expressed in specific situations or contexts. Think of brand voice as the overarching identity, while tone adjusts based on the content or channel used to convey the message.

Why does brand voice matter?

In today's crowded digital landscape, where every brand competes for attention, having a distinct and consistent voice is essential for standing out and being memorable. While visual elements like logos and design play a significant role, it's the brand voice that humanizes interaction and builds a deeper emotional connection with the audience. Follow these steps to establish a strong brand voice:

1. **Review your company's mission statement:** This serves as the foundation for your brand voice, aligning it with your core values and goals.

2. **Audit your current content & messaging:** Analyze existing content across all communication channels to identify inconsistencies and determine what resonates with your audience.

3. **Research your audience:** Understand your target demographic, their preferences, language, and interests, and tailor your brand voice accordingly.

4. **Do a "We're this, not that" exercise:** Define your brand personality by contrasting it with what it is not, helping to clarify your unique voice.

5. **Create a brand voice chart:** Document key elements of your brand voice, including tone, style, and messaging guidelines, to stay consistent.

6. **Enforce consistency with clearly documented guidelines:** Develop a comprehensive brand style guide that outlines your brand voice principles and provides examples for reference.

Tips for developing a strong brand voice:

Identify your audience and personas: Tailor your brand voice to resonate with your target demographic by understanding their characteristics and preferences.

Audit your current tone and voice: Analyze existing content to identify patterns and inconsistencies and refine your brand voice accordingly.

Tailor your tone to different content and channels: Adjust your brand voice based on the context and platform to maintain relevance and effectiveness.

Document everything and be consistent: Create a brand style guide to maintain consistency in tone, style, and messaging across all channels and content types.

Monitor, review, and adapt: Regularly review and refine your brand voice based on audience feedback and evolving trends to stay relevant and engaging.

Examples of top brand voices, such as Fenty Beauty, Oatly, and Slack, demonstrate how brands effectively leverage distinct personalities to connect with their audience. Whether it's Fenty Beauty's bold and authentic tone, Oatly's quirky and humorous approach, or Slack's clear and concise communication, each brand's voice reflects its unique identity and resonates with its target demographic.

The Visual Impact

Visual branding plays a crucial role in establishing a brand's identity and creating a memorable impression on its audience. Building a brand is not just about crafting a compelling story or message. Visual elements are equally important in capturing attention and building recognition. Let's delve into the significance of visual brand identity and how to make it stand out:

Visual brand identity: Visual brand identity encompasses all the visual components that represent how a brand is perceived. It goes beyond colors and design, encompassing elements such as logos, color palettes, fonts, and imagery. Consistency in visual identity is key to resonating effectively with the audience and reinforcing brand recognition.

Benefits of visual marketing: In today's visually driven marketing landscape, incorporating visuals into your marketing strategy is essential for long-term success. Visuals are highly effective in capturing attention, conveying brand personality, and making a lasting impression on the audience.

Essential visual branding elements

- **Logo**: A well-designed logo is essential for brand recognition and should reflect the brand's personality.

- **Color palette**: Consistent use of colors across all brand assets helps create brand recognition and association.

- **Fonts**: Fonts should align with the brand's personality and resonate with the target audience.

- **Imagery**: Images should be relevant to the brand and resonate with the audience, evoking emotions and enhancing brand perception.

- **Layout**: How visual elements are arranged and presented plays a significant role in brand recognition and user experience.

Tips for Creating a Strong Visual Brand Identity

Be unique: Stand out from the competition by understanding competitors' visual identities and crafting a distinct visual style.

Be memorable: Aim to create visuals that are instantly recognizable and associated with your brand, even without context.

Ensure consistency: Maintain consistency across all visual elements to create a cohesive brand identity.

Understand your audience: Tailor visual elements to resonate with your target audience's preferences and perceptions.

How to Create Good Visuals

Get your logo right: Invest time in designing a logo that reflects your brand's personality and is memorable.

Choose a consistent color palette: Use consistent colors across all brand assets to reinforce brand recognition.

Select fonts wisely: Choose fonts that align with your brand's personality and appeal to your audience.

Use relevant imagery: Select images that are relevant to your brand and evoke the desired emotions in your audience.

Consider layout: Pay attention to how visual elements are arranged to ensure a cohesive and visually appealing presentation.

Evoke emotions: Use visuals to create an emotional connection with your audience and reinforce brand affinity.

By understanding the importance of visual branding and implementing effective visual elements, brands can create a strong visual identity that resonates with their audience and sets them apart from competitors.

Summary

In this chapter, we dove into the essential pillars of advertising, branding, and marketing, laying a sturdy foundation for any business endeavor. From understanding the core principles to mastering the art of crafting a compelling brand identity, we explored how these elements work synergistically to elevate your business and captivate your audience. I emphasized the significance of cultivating a robust online presence in today's digital landscape, offering insights and strategies to help you navigate and thrive in the ever-evolving online sphere.

Key takeaways include the importance of:

- **Mastering the fundamentals**: Understanding the principles of advertising, branding, and marketing is crucial for strategic business promotion.

- **Building a compelling brand presence**: Crafting a unique brand identity that resonates with your target audience is vital for long-term success.

- **Leveraging online platforms**: Harnessing the power of the internet to establish and expand your brand's presence is essential in today's digital age.

As we turn the page, get ready to go deeper into the realm of marketing. Our next chapter is packed with practical insights and actionable strategies that empower you to confidently navigate the competitive marketplace. From guerrilla tactics to digital marketing mastery, I've got you covered. Get ready to elevate your marketing game and propel your business to new heights!

Chapter 9
Marketing Made Easier

*Business has only two functions—marketing and
innovation.*

–Milan Kundera

T HIS INSIGHTFUL QUOTE ABOVE captures the essence
of what drives business success. This chapter explores
the first of these crucial functions: marketing. Effective marketing is the lifeblood of any business, enabling entrepreneurs
to reach and engage their target audience.

Through practical insights and actionable strategies, this
chapter equips you with the tools you need to promote your
business effectively. You will learn how to navigate the competitive marketplace with confidence, ensuring your marketing efforts stand out and resonate with potential customers.
Whether you are launching a new venture or looking to in-
vigorate an existing one, the strategies discussed here will help
you harness the power of marketing to fuel your business's
growth and success.

Creating a Marketing Strategy

An effective marketing strategy is crucial for any business.
However, many companies make common mistakes that hinder their success. This section highlights those mistakes and
guides on building a unique and successful marketing strategy.

Importance of an Effective Marketing Strategy

A highly effective marketing strategy is crucial to your business because it introduces your brand to your target audience and converts individuals into customers. It is the primary source of revenue for your business, generating consistent cash flow.

The first objective of any marketing strategy is to enhance brand awareness. It should make your business more recognizable and deepen your customer's understanding of your product or service. Your marketing messages should encourage customer loyalty and interaction by boosting their engagement with your brand.

The best marketing plans include a deep understanding of your target market, providing insights into customer needs and preferences. The ability to pinpoint the most relevant customer segments enhances the effectiveness of your marketing campaigns and improves conversion rates.

A successful marketing strategy differentiates your business from competitors and strengthens brand recognition through consistently memorable brand presence. The ultimate goal is to elevate sales and increase revenue. This is achieved through targeted marketing that converts prospects into paying customers.

Crafting a Winning Marketing Strategy

For a business to thrive, it must have a meticulously crafted marketing strategy. This serves as the guiding framework to attain objectives and effectively connect with the intended audience. This strategy entails more than just inventive concepts; it necessitates a profound comprehension of market dynamics, the competitive landscape, and the customers' evolving needs. It acts as a detailed map, delineating the methodologies and platforms essential for engaging with the target clientele.

In this comprehensive guide, we dive into the fundamental elements of a resilient marketing strategy. Here I provide a systematic approach to developing a strategy that harmonizes with your business aspirations. In addition, I underscore the significance of actively monitoring progress and making timely adjustments to ensure the strategy remains pertinent and fruitful.

Step 1: Understand the Market and Target Audience

The first step in building a successful marketing strategy is understanding the market and identifying your target audience. This involves researching customer demographics and behaviors, as well as analyzing the competition:

- **Demographic Research**: This entails gathering detailed consumer information, including age, gender, income, and geographic location. This data helps you create a profile of your ideal customer, allowing you to tailor your marketing efforts to resonate with them. Methods include conducting surveys, analyzing website and social media data, and reviewing industry reports.

- **Behavioral Study**: It's imperative to understand how customers interact with your brand, their purchasing habits, and decision-making processes. Methods such as purchase history analysis, website analytics, and social media listening provide valuable insights into customer behavior.

- **Competitor Analysis**: Analyzing your competitors' strategies and identifying their strengths and weaknesses helps you find opportunities to differentiate your brand. Techniques like SWOT (Strengths, Weaknesses, Opportunities, and Threats) analysis and benchmarking are useful for this purpose.

Step 2: Set Measurable Objectives

Setting measurable objectives is crucial for tracking the success of your marketing efforts. These objectives should be SMART: Specific, Measurable, Achievable, Relevant, and Time-bound:

- **Specific**: Clearly defined goals, such as "increase sales by 10% in the next quarter."

- **Measurable**: Objectives should have quantifiable criteria, like "increase website traffic by 20% in the next month."

- **Achievable**: Goals should be realistic. Example: increasing sales by 20% next year

- **Relevant**: Ensure objectives align with your overall business strategy, like increasing brand awareness to support a new product launch.

- **Time-bound**: Set deadlines for achieving your goals, for example, "increase social media followers by 50% by the end of the month."

Step 3: Develop a Messaging Framework

A messaging framework ensures consistent and cohesive communication with your target audience across all marketing channels.

- **Key messages**: Develop a set of key messages to highlight your unique value proposition. These should be memorable, compelling, and aligned with your business strategy.

- **Audience-centric**: Tailor your messages to the needs and preferences of your target audience. Use market research and customer feedback to understand their pain points.

- **Benefit-focused**: Emphasize the benefits of your products or services rather than just the features. This approach creates a stronger emotional connection with your audience.

Step 4: Choose the Right Marketing Channels

Selecting the appropriate marketing channels is essential for reaching your audience effectively.

- **Understand your audience**: Determine where your target audience spends their time, whether on social media platforms, industry publications, or other channels.

- **Align with objectives**: Choose channels that match your marketing objectives. For example, social media may be best for brand awareness, while email marketing could be more effective for driving conversions.

- **Consider budget and resources**: Focus on channels that offer the best return on investment and are feasible within your budget and resources.

Step 5: Develop a Content Strategy

A robust content strategy is vital for attracting and engaging your target audience.

- **Identify relevant topics**: Research your audience's interests and pain points to create content that addresses their needs.

- **Choose effective formats**: Select content formats that resonate with your audience, such as videos, blog posts, infographics, or podcasts.

- **Distribute on suitable channels**: Share your content on platforms where your audience is most active, including social media, blogs, and email campaigns.

- **Focus on quality**: Prioritize creating high-quality content that provides value, establishes leadership, and builds trust with your audience.

Step 6: Measure and Adjust

Continuous monitoring and evaluation are crucial for the success of your marketing strategy.

- **Track Key Performance Indicators (KPIs)**: Measure metrics. These include website traffic, conversion rates, ROI, social media engagement, and customer retention.

- **Analyze data**: Use data analysis to gain insights into your marketing efforts' effectiveness and identify areas for improvement.

- **Adjust strategy**: Based on your findings, make necessary adjustments to optimize your marketing tactics and better cater to your target audience.

Step 7: Embrace a Dynamic Approach

A successful marketing strategy must be adaptable to changing market conditions and customer needs.

- **Ongoing market research**: Regularly conduct market research to stay updated with industry trends and customer preferences.

- **Adapt to changes**: Be prepared to adjust your strategy in response to unexpected events or shifts in the market, ensuring your marketing efforts remain relevant and effective.

Follow these steps and continuously refine your approach to create a comprehensive marketing strategy that drives growth and helps achieve your business objectives.

Mistakes to Avoid in Your Marketing Strategy

Creating a successful digital marketing strategy is crucial for the growth and prosperity of any contemporary business. Increasingly, consumers are turning to the Internet for their shopping needs. A solid digital marketing plan is indispensable for drawing in new customers and keeping current ones loyal. Nevertheless, developing this strategy is complex and fraught with potential errors that many businesses commonly make.

To assist you in navigating these challenges, I have identified and outlined the most frequent mistakes to avoid in your digital marketing efforts. Although developing a high-performing digital marketing strategy can be difficult, it is essential for succeeding in the competitive landscape of today's market:

Lack of clear goals:

Without specific, measurable goals, your strategy lacks direction. Ensure your objectives are well-defined and align with your overall business goals.

Ignoring your target audience:

Knowing your target audience is essential. Skipping the research needed to understand their needs, preferences, and behaviors can lead to ineffective marketing.

Emphasizing sales over brand building:

Focusing too heavily on sales at the expense of building your brand can undermine long-term success. Balance sales efforts with strategies that enhance your brand's image and value.

Underestimating the power of data:

Data-driven decisions are crucial for optimizing your strategy. Neglecting to track and analyze data means missing opportunities for informed adjustments and improvements.

Insufficient Idea Generation:

Failing to brainstorm enough ideas can lead to stale and uninspired marketing campaigns. Encourage creativity and continuous idea generation to keep your strategy fresh.

Believing in a Perfect Moment for Marketing:

Waiting for an ideal time to market can result in missed opportunities. Marketing should be continuous, adaptable to changing conditions, and ready to seize opportunities as they arise.

The Power of Social Media

Why Utilize Social Media Marketing

Enhance brand visibility:

Social media platforms provide an excellent opportunity to boost your brand's visibility. By crafting and sharing engaging content, you increase the chances of your brand being seen by a broader audience.

Expand your customer reach:

Reaching new customers can be challenging, but social media levels the playing field. It enables small businesses to connect with a wider audience through targeted content and ads.

Gain deeper customer Insights:

Social media offers valuable data about your customers' interests, behaviors, and needs, helping you tailor your marketing efforts to meet their expectations.

Monitor your competitors:

Your competitors are likely active on social media. Observing their strategies can provide insights into what works and what doesn't, allowing you to refine your approach.

Foster long-term customer relationships:

Building strong relationships with your customers is crucial. Engaging with them through social media helps establish trust and loyalty, encouraging repeat business and positive word-of-mouth.

Choosing the Best Social Media Platforms for Your Business

Facebook

- **Audience**: Diverse, from young adults to older generations.

- **Advantages**: Multi-use platform for ads, pages, and e-commerce shops. Ideal for businesses targeting a broad demographic.

- **Best for** businesses aiming to build an all-encompassing social media presence.

Instagram

- **Audience**: Primarily 18–34 years old.

- **Advantages**: Highly visual platform, perfect for industries like fashion, food, and travel. In-app shopping features enhance e-commerce capabilities.

- **Best for** brands with strong visual content and a

younger target audience.

Twitter

- **Audience**: Broad, with significant engagement from users aged 16–64.

- **Advantages**: Real-time engagement, conversational tone, and hashtag usage to increase content visibility.

- **Best for** businesses focusing on quick updates, customer service, and trending topics.

TikTok

- **Audience**: Predominantly 18–24 years old.

- **Advantages**: High potential for virality and creative content. Suitable for brands willing to experiment and think outside the box.

- **Best for** brands targeting younger audiences with creative video content.

Pinterest

- **Audience**: Majority women, particularly 25–34 years old.

- **Advantages**: Positive, highly visual platform. Excellent for driving traffic and sales through visually appealing pins.

- **Best for** businesses in home decor, fashion, and DIY industries.

YouTube

- **Audience**: Wide-ranging, highly engaged.

- **Advantages**: Great for detailed content and improving SEO. High potential for building brand awareness through engaging videos.

- **Best for** brands capable of producing high-quality video content.

Social Media Best Practices for Small Businesses

Plan your content ahead of time:

Avoid last-minute stress by creating a social media content calendar. Plan and organize your posts to maintain a consistent and varied content mix.

Schedule your posts:

Utilize scheduling tools to automate your posts, ensuring they go live at optimal times without disrupting your workflow.

Engage in community management:

Actively interact with your audience by responding to comments, answering questions, and participating in conversations. This fosters a sense of community and strengthens customer relationships.

Stay current with trends:

Keep an eye on social media trends to understand what your audience is interested in. This helps in creating relevant and engaging content.

Leverage social commerce:

Utilize social media's e-commerce features to sell your products directly on platforms like Facebook, Instagram, and Pinterest, reducing friction in the purchasing process.

Utilize analytics for future planning:

Analyze your social media performance to identify successful content types and strategies. Use this data to refine your future posts and focus on platforms that yield the best results.

By following these guidelines and choosing the right platforms, you can effectively leverage social media to grow your small business and engage with your target audience.

Social Media Management Tools

Buffer:

Buffer is ideal for straightforward social media scheduling. It supports various platforms, including X (formerly Twitter), LinkedIn, Facebook, Instagram, Mastodon, TikTok, Google

Business Profile, and Pinterest. Buffer offers a free plan with limited features and more comprehensive plans starting at $6 per month per social channel. Its key features include:

- Easy-to-use scheduling for multiple social media accounts

- A "link in bio" service called Start Page for quick mobile-friendly site creation

- Integration with Shopify to track the impact of social posts on store performance

- An AI assistant for generating and rephrasing posts

Hootsuite:

Hootsuite is a fully featured social media management platform, particularly strong for managing X. It supports scheduling, inbox monitoring, and managing posts across Facebook, YouTube, Instagram, LinkedIn, TikTok, and Pinterest. Starting at $99 per month, it offers:

- Comprehensive analytics with industry comparisons

- Best-in-class X integration

- AI-powered content generation with OwlyWriter AI

- Extensive team and collaboration tools

SocialPilot:

SocialPilot is tailored for small teams, offering robust features at an affordable price. Supporting X, Facebook, Instagram, YouTube, LinkedIn, TikTok, Pinterest, Google Business Profile, and Tumblr, it starts at $30 per month. Highlights include:

- Cost-effective team management features

- Roles and permissions for content approval workflows

- Basic but functional user interface

- AI assistant for content creation

Loomly:

Loomly is notable for its custom social network feature that allows posting to almost any service via Zapier. It includes separate scheduling calendars for different social media needs and starts at $42 per month. Key features are:

- Custom Channel for posting to various platforms

- Scheduling for multiple social media accounts

- Basic scheduling, inbox management, and analytics

Iconosquare:

Iconosquare excels with visual social networks like Instagram and TikTok. It offers detailed Instagram analytics and scheduling options, starting at $39 per month. Features include:

- Scheduling for Instagram photos, carousels, Reels, and Stories

- Cross-posting capabilities

- Comprehensive Instagram analytics and social listening

Sendible:

Sendible is a cost-effective all-in-one social media management tool supporting Instagram, Facebook, TikTok, LinkedIn, Google Business Profile, YouTube, WordPress, and X. Starting at $29 per month, it provides:

- Affordable pricing with essential features

- Quick reports on social media performance

- Integration with Google Analytics for traffic analysis

- Basic but efficient scheduling and inbox management

Choosing the Right Tool

When selecting a social media management tool, consider the
following features:

- **Support for multiple platforms**: Ensure the tool
  supports all your required social networks.

- **Scheduling capabilities**: Look for powerful scheduling tools to batch your posts.

- **Analytics**: The tool should offer detailed analytics to
  measure your social media performance.

- **Cost-effectiveness**: Evaluate the pricing against the
  features offered to ensure value for money.

- **Team collaboration**: If you have a team, opt for
  tools with robust collaboration and approval workflows.

- **AI features**: Some tools offer AI capabilities for content generation and optimization, enhancing efficiency.

Working With Influencers

Influencer marketing leverages individuals with substantial social media followings to promote products or services. Here's a quick guide to its benefits:

- **Build credibility**: Influencers have dedicated, trusting followers. Their endorsements can instantly boost your brand's credibility.

- **Create engaging content**: Influencers craft content that resonates with their audience, making your brand's message more compelling.

- **Reach target audiences**: Collaborate with influencers in your niche to reach a broader and more relevant audience.

- **Increase website traffic**: Influencers can drive followers to your website through links and special promotions.

- **Boost sales**: Personal endorsements from influencers can significantly enhance your sales by adding trust and authenticity.

- **Generate content**: Influencers produce high-quality, diverse content you can repurpose across your marketing channels.

By strategically using influencer marketing, you can effectively connect with your audience, enhance content, and drive business growth.

Types of Social Media Influencers

- **Nano-influencers**

  - Have up to 10,000 followers

  - **Example**: Lindsay Gallimore, a mommy blogger with 7.8K followers.

- **Micro-influencers**

  - Have between 10,000 and 100,000 followers

  - Example: Sharon Mendelaoui, a lifestyle blogger with 12.3K followers.

- **Macro-influencers**

  - Have 100,000 to 1 million followers

  - **Example**: Jean Lee, a food and travel creator with 109K followers.

- **Mega-influencers**

  - Have over 1 million followers

  - **Example**: Savannah LaBrant, a TikTok star with

30.3M followers.

Influencer Marketing Strategies

Choose the right influencer:

Select influencers whose values align with your brand and whose followers match your target demographic.

Understand the different levels of influence:

Different influencers (nano, micro, macro, and mega) offer varying reach and engagement, influencing your strategy and budget.

Decide how to reach out to them:

Engage with their content organically before sending a personalized direct message or email to propose a partnership.

Determine what you want to achieve:

Define clear objectives such as increasing brand awareness, driving traffic, or boosting sales to measure the campaign's success.

Build a genuine relationship with the influencer:

Allow influencers creative freedom to ensure their endorsements are authentic and resonate well with their audience.

Mastering Search Engine Marketing (SEM)

Search engine marketing enhances a website's visibility on search engines through paid ads (SEM) and optimization techniques (SEO). SEM involves paying for top placements on search results pages:

Benefits of search engine marketing

- **Increase brand awareness**: SEM boosts brand visibility by placing ads at the top of search results, increasing recognition even without clicks.

- **Fast results**: Unlike SEO, SEM provides immediate visibility by bidding on keywords, driving instant traffic and conversions.

- **Boost traffic**: Target specific keywords to attract a relevant audience, increasing website visits and engagement.

- **Easy to manage**: SEM platforms offer user-friendly tools for efficient campaign management, allowing easy adjustments based on performance.

- **Measurable results**: Track impressions, clicks, CTR, and conversions to assess and improve campaign effectiveness.

- **More leads**: Attract highly qualified leads by targeting specific search queries, increasing the likelihood of conversion.

- **Pay after interaction**: Pay only when someone interacts with your ad, maximizing budget efficiency and exposure.

- **Reach clients instantly**: Gain immediate exposure with SEM, ideal for time-sensitive promotions and rapid audience engagement.

- **Targeted audiences**: Precisely target audiences based on demographics, location, and search behavior, ensuring relevance and higher conversion rates.

Key Elements of Search Engine Marketing

Local SEO:

Local SEO focuses on optimizing your online presence to attract local customers. This involves managing your Google My Business profile, ensuring your business information is consistent across online directories, and collecting customer reviews to improve your visibility in local search results.

Keywords:

Keywords are the terms and phrases potential customers use to search for products or services. Effective keyword research helps you identify the most relevant terms to target, allowing you to optimize your content and ads to attract the right audience and improve your search engine rankings.

Social media marketing:

Social media marketing leverages platforms like Facebook, Instagram, and Twitter to promote your business and engage with your audience. This strategy enhances your brand visibility and supports your SEM efforts by driving additional traffic to your website.

Content:

Creating high-quality, relevant, and valuable content is essential for attracting and retaining your target audience. Good content helps improve your search engine rankings and can be used in organic SEO and paid SEM strategies to drive traffic and conversions.

Pay-Per-Click Advertising (PPC)

PPC is a paid advertising model where you pay each time someone clicks on your ad. These ads appear at the top of search engine results pages, providing instant visibility and driving targeted traffic to your site. PPC campaigns can be tailored to specific keywords and audiences to maximize effectiveness.

Content marketing:

Content marketing involves creating and distributing valuable content to attract and engage your audience. This supports SEM by improving your site's relevance and authority, leading to better search engine rankings and increased traffic.

Content optimization:

Content optimization ensures your content is easily discoverable by search engines and provides a great user experience. This involves using the right keywords, ensuring fast load times, and creating a seamless navigation experience to keep visitors engaged and improve your rankings.

Landing pages:

Landing pages are specialized web pages designed for specific marketing campaigns. They are optimized to convert visitors into leads or customers by focusing on a single call to action and providing relevant information that matches the user's search intent.

Search intent:

Understanding search intent means identifying the purpose behind a user's search query. By aligning your content and ads with the user's intent, you can improve relevance and increase the chances of conversion, ensuring that your SEM efforts are more effective.

Keyword Research

Keyword research identifies and analyzes the search terms people enter into search engines. That data is used to guide content creation and marketing strategies.

Keyword research is crucial because it helps you understand what your target audience is searching for. By targeting these keywords, you can create content that aligns with the searchers' needs, thereby increasing your visibility on search engines, driving more traffic to your site, and ultimately improving your conversion rates.

Elements of Keyword Research

- **Relevance**: Your content must meet the search intent of users and provide valuable information that matches their queries.

- **Authority**: Your website should be seen as a credible source. This involves producing high-quality content and earning backlinks from other authoritative sites.

- **Volume**: The monthly search volume (MSV) indicates how often a keyword is searched. Higher-volume keywords can drive more traffic, but they are usually more competitive.

How to Find and Choose Keywords for Your Website

Step 1: **Use Google Keyword Planner to refine your list**: Utilize Google Keyword Planner to get search volume and traffic estimates for your keywords. Google Trends can help you identify the trending keywords worth focusing on.

Step 2: **Prioritize keywords that are easier to rank for**: Focus on "low-hanging fruit" keywords with lower competition and are within your website's authority to rank for.

Step 3: **Check the monthly search volume (MSV) for your selected keywords**: Use tools like searchvolume.io or Google Trends to determine the monthly search volume and ensure you target keywords that people are actively searching for.

Step 4: **Consider SERP features when selecting keywords**: Look for SERP features like image packs, paragraph snippets, list snippets, and video snippets. Tailor your content to fit these features to increase your chances of being highlighted in search results.

Step 5: **Ensure a mix of head terms and long-tail keywords**: Balance your keyword strategy with head terms (short, generic phrases) and long-tail keywords (longer, more specific phrases) to capture both high-volume searches and more specific, lower-competition queries.

Step 6: **Analyze competitors' keyword rankings**: Investigate which keywords your competitors are ranking for. This can help you identify valuable keywords to target and reveal opportunities where you can outperform them.

SEO: Improve Your Search Engine Rankings

- **Understand your online customers**: Know the stages of customer search behavior (Awareness, Consideration, Purchase) to target relevant keywords effectively.

- **Use keywords on your website**: Naturally incorporate relevant keywords into titles, content, and metadata to improve SEO without keyword stuffing.

- **Update your content regularly**: Frequent updates encourage search engines to index your site more often. Add new content like product updates and customer stories. Refresh existing content every six months.

- **Gain referrals from other websites**: Backlinks from reputable sites signal trustworthiness to search engines. Focus on getting links from high-authority websites.

- **Use meta tags**: Utilize meta descriptions, title tags, and alt text to provide search engines with additional information about your content.

- **Stay current with SEO trends**: Monitor changes in search engine algorithms, new keywords, and search technologies to keep your SEO strategy effective.

With these strategies, you can boost your search engine rankings and increase your website's visibility. Improve your search engine rankings and increase the visibility of your business online.

Setting Up a Paid Search Campaign

Paid search vs organic search

Paid search ads appear at the top of SERPs due to payment, while organic search results are ranked based on SEO efforts.

Benefits of paid search advertising

Paid search offers immediate visibility, precise targeting, measurable results, and enhanced control over ad campaigns.

How Paid Search Advertising Works

Advertisers bid on keywords, and their ads appear on SERPs based on the bid amount and ad relevance. Payment occurs per click (PPC).

Types of Paid Search Ads

- **Text Ads**: Basic ads that appear on SERPs.

- **Shopping Ads**: Showcase products with images and prices.

- **Display Ads**: Visual ads shown on partner websites.

- **Video Ads**: Ads that appear on video platforms like YouTube.

- **App promotion Ads**: Promote mobile apps.

Steps to Launch and Manage Your Paid Search Campaign

1. **Set up your Google Ads account:** Visit Google Ads and create an account. Start your first campaign.

2. **Choose a campaign name and type:** Select "Search Network Only" for beginners. Name your campaign based on the advertised product or service.

3. **Define Ad display locations**: Target specific locations where your audience is likely to be, such as a city or country.

4. **Set a daily budget**: Start with a low daily budget to gather data and adjust as needed.

5. **Add keywords**: Focus on high-intent keywords potential buyers would use. Avoid adding too many keywords initially.

6. **Create your Ad**: Craft compelling ads with relevant keywords, clear benefits, and a strong call to action. Link it to a targeted landing page.

7. **Set up conversion tracking**: Implement tracking for webform leads, calls, e-commerce orders, or offline sales to measure ad effectiveness.

8. **Monitor and optimize**: Regularly review analytics to identify successful ads and optimize your campaign for better ROI.

Follow these steps, to effectively launch and manage your paid search marketing campaign to drive targeted traffic and improve conversions.

Email Marketing Isn't Dead

Email marketing is a strategic approach involving sending emails to current and potential customers to enhance brand awareness, drive engagement, nurture leads, and boost sales. Given the global email user base exceeding 4 billion, businesses can't afford to overlook this powerful communication tool. In 2022, email marketing boasted an impressive ROI of $36 for every $1 spent.

What is the Benefit of Email Marketing?

Here are the top six:

1. **Enhance brand awareness**: Email marketing enables businesses to share valuable resources, news, updates, and educational content, aligning email content and design with the brand identity to reinforce brand awareness.

2. **Boost website traffic**: By including snippets of recent articles or promotional calls to action, emails can direct subscribers to the website, increasing traffic to blogs, landing pages, and sales pages.

3. **Drive sales and revenue**: Emails can highlight products and services, offer discounts, or use upselling techniques, encouraging purchases and increasing revenue.

4. **Support other marketing channels**: Email marketing can drive traffic to other channels, such as social media and blogs, and promote events, creating a cohesive omnichannel strategy.

5. **Maintain customer engagement**: Diverse email campaigns keep customers interested and engaged with the brand, helping maintain a continuous relationship and staying top-of-mind.

6. **Collect valuable business data**: Tracking email analytics and collecting feedback through surveys can provide insights into customer behavior, enabling data-driven decisions to improve business strategies.

Types of Email Marketing Campaigns and Examples

Welcome emails:

These introduce new subscribers to your brand, often achieving high open rates. For instance, Duolingo's welcome email focuses on helping new users continue their language studies.

Newsletter emails:

Typically non-promotional, newsletters share industry news, tips, and updates. Visme's newsletter, for example, highlights blog content on brand visual design.

Promotional email campaigns:

These aim to promote specific products or sales. Modernica's Black Friday email is a good example, showcasing top sales items to entice customers.

Cart abandonment emails:

Sent to remind shoppers about abandoned carts, these emails can recover potential sales, like Public Rec's cart abandonment email.

Seasonal marketing campaigns:

These align with specific seasons or holidays to promote relevant products. Lush's Halloween-themed email is a prime example.

Other Campaign types

- **Re-engagement emails**: Attempt to re-engage inactive subscribers.

- **Announcement emails**: Notify subscribers about new products or events.

- **Triggered email series**: Based on customer actions, like the welcome or cart abandonment series.

- **Post-purchase drip**: Sent after purchase to enhance the customer experience and encourage future purchases.

- **Connect-via-social campaigns**: Encourage subscribers to follow on social media.

- **Testimonial request emails**: Request feedback and reviews from customers.

How to Send Marketing Emails

1. **Implement email segmentation**: Group your email list based on demographics, purchase history, or engagement levels to send targeted messages.

2. **A/B test your marketing emails**: Test different versions of emails to determine what works best, such as subject lines, images, or CTAs.

3. **Analyze your email marketing performance**: Track metrics like open rates, click-through rates, and conversions to assess email effectiveness.

4. **Set email marketing KPIs**: Define key performance indicators to measure the success of your campaigns, such as subscriber growth, ROI, or engagement rates.

5. **Adjust email components to improve results**: Based on performance data, tweak email elements like design, content, or timing to optimize results.

6. **Use an email marketing report template**: Regularly review performance using standardized templates to track progress and identify areas for improvement.

How to Build an Email Marketing List

- **Place Opt-in forms around your website**: Embed sign-up forms on your home page, blog, and landing pages to capture visitor emails.

- **Create gated content and lead magnets**: Offer valuable content like eBooks or templates in exchange for email addresses.

- **Use event sign-up forms**: Require email registration for webinars or in-person events to build your list.

Tips to Create a Successful Email Marketing Campaign

Choose a relevant email list: Ensure emails are sent to the right audience, avoiding unethical practices like buying email lists.

Design your email: Create visually appealing emails that align with your brand, include white space, and use images and responsive design.

Personalize your email subject line and content: Use subscriber data to tailor emails, mentioning names, locations, or preferences.

Be conversational: Write in a friendly, relatable tone to engage subscribers and build relationships.

Create follow-ups: Develop a series of emails to nurture leads, such as abandoned cart reminders or welcome series.

Send emails from a real person: Use recognizable sender names to appear more personal and trustworthy.

A/B test your emails: Experiment with different email versions to optimize performance.

Follow email or spam regulations: Comply with regulations like the CAN-SPAM Act and GDPR to avoid penalties.

Track the success of your email campaigns: Monitor key metrics to understand what's working and make data-driven improvements.

Trade Show Marketing

Trade show marketing involves participating in industry-specific events to showcase your products and services. It boosts brand visibility, helps you meet potential customers, network with industry professionals, and stay updated on market trends.

Why attend trade shows?

- **Boost brand awareness**: Increase your visibility and make your brand memorable.

- **Gather customer feedback**: Gain insights directly from customers about your products.

- **Competitive analysis**: Observe competitors and learn from their strategies.

- **Vendor connections**: Meet vendors who can offer beneficial products or services.

- **Generate leads**: Every attendee is a potential lead.

Tips for a successful trade show

- **Set clear goals**: Define what you want to achieve, like generating leads or increasing sales.

- **Choose relevant shows**: Attend trade shows that align with your industry and target audience.

- **Prepare thoroughly**: Bring all necessary materials, including business cards, promotional items, and product samples.

- **Engage actively**: Interact with attendees, demonstrate products, and build connections.

- **Follow up**: After the event, send personalized emails to the contacts you made.

Examples of effective strategies

- **Product showcases**: Use live demonstrations to attract attention.

- **Interactive booths**: Provide hands-on experiences to engage visitors.

- **Networking events**: Host small events at your booth to foster industry connections.

By preparing well and engaging actively, trade show marketing can significantly enhance your brand and drive business growth.

Measuring Success

Evaluating marketing strategies through metrics is crucial for optimizing campaigns, cutting costs, and increasing profits. Proper analysis tools help assess the impact of campaigns, ensuring goals are met effectively. Tracking key performance indicators (KPIs) in marketing is essential to understand market demands and customer needs.

Key benefits include:

- **Satisfaction levels**: Gauge customer contentment.

- **Retention rates**: Measure customer loyalty.

- **Training costs**: Assess expenses for staff training.

- **Acquisition and profitability**: Evaluate the cost-effectiveness of acquiring new customers.

KPIs in Marketing

- **Sales growth**: Measures revenue increases attributed to marketing efforts.

- **Lead generation**: Tracks the number of potential customers acquired.

- **Customer Lifetime Value (LTV)**: Estimates the total revenue a business can expect from a customer over their lifetime

- **Cost of Customer Acquisition (COCA)**: Calculates the expense of gaining a new customer

- **Sales team response time**: Measures the promptness of responses to leads

- **Website traffic to lead ratio**: Determines the percentage of website visitors converting into leads

- **Lead to Marketing Qualified Lead (MQL) ratio**: Evaluates the quality of leads by tracking those that become MQLs

- **MQL to Sales Qualified Lead (SQL) ratio**: Measures the transition from MQLs to SQLs, indicating collaboration between marketing and sales

Regularly monitoring these KPIs ensures that marketing strategies are aligned with business objectives and continuously improved for better results.

Summary

This chapter provides entrepreneurs with practical insights and actionable strategies to enhance their marketing efforts. By measuring the success of marketing strategies through KPIs, businesses can optimize their campaigns, save costs, and generate higher profits. Key metrics such as sales growth, lead generation, customer lifetime value, cost of customer acquisition, and conversion ratios between different stages of the sales funnel are essential for understanding and improving marketing performance. You are now equipped with tools to implement, control, and refine your marketing strategies, ensuring they achieve their established objectives and stay competitive in the marketplace.

In the next chapter, we will jump into strategies for scaling your business to achieve sustained growth. Building on the marketing foundations laid out in this chapter, we will explore advanced techniques and best practices for expanding your market reach, increasing operational efficiency, and driving long-term profitability. Get ready to uncover the secrets to taking your business to the next level and ensuring its success in the competitive landscape. Stay tuned as I guide you through the critical steps and strategies necessary for successful business scaling, providing you with the knowledge and confidence to navigate this exciting phase of your entrepreneurial journey.

Chapter 10
Scaling Your Business

Don't sit down and wait for the opportunities to come. Get up and make them.
 —Madam C.J. Walker

T HIS POWERFUL QUOTE ABOVE encapsulates the proactive mindset necessary for entrepreneurial success. In the dynamic business world, waiting for opportunities is not an option. Instead, entrepreneurs must take deliberate and strategic actions to create opportunities and drive growth. This chapter equips you with practical insights and actionable strategies to scale your business effectively, ensuring sustained growth and a competitive edge in the marketplace. Scaling a business is a complex and multifaceted process that involves more than just increasing sales or expanding operations. It requires a deep understanding of your market, robust operational frameworks, and a strategic resource management approach.

In this chapter, you will learn how to identify and seize growth opportunities, optimize your operations for efficiency, and implement strategies to sustainably grow your business. Whether you're looking to expand your customer base, enter new markets, or enhance your product offerings, the insights, and strategies outlined in this chapter will provide the tools and knowledge needed to take your business to the next level. By the end of this chapter, you will be well-equipped to navigate the challenges of scaling and poised to achieve long-term success.

Scaling a Business

What does scaling a business mean?

Scaling a business is often misunderstood, so let me clarify what it truly entails and how it differs from mere business growth.

Growth vs. scaling up

- **Business growth**: Growth is generally seen as a linear process where a company increases its resources—such as capital, personnel, or technology—and in turn, its revenue grows. For example, an advertising agency gaining more clients would need to hire additional staff to handle the increased workload, leading to higher revenue but also higher costs. This type of growth is resource-intensive and can strain a company's finances.

- **Scaling**: In contrast, scaling refers to increasing revenue without corresponding significantly increased costs. A company achieves scaling when its operations can handle increased business volume. For instance, an insurance company that adopts a cloud-based phone system can manage more customers without hiring additional staff, thereby increasing revenue without a proportional rise in expenses. Essentially, scaling involves optimizing processes so they can handle larger volumes seamlessly.

When is it time to scale?

Growing a company requires careful timing. Here are key signs that indicate it's time to expand your business:

Rising sales: Consistently increasing sales suggest it's time to invest in scaling to meet market demand.

Need for specialized leadership: Requiring more specialized leaders in IT, finance, legal, and sales indicates growth. Bringing in expertise helps manage expansion effectively.

Employees seeking growth: If your team is looking for career advancement, scaling can provide new opportunities and keep them motivated.

Exceeding capacity: When demand consistently outstrips your resources, it's time to expand to avoid turning away business and missing deadlines.

Decision-making bottlenecks: If you are in a bottleneck in decision-making, delegate more responsibilities to streamline operations and enable growth.

Leadership focus on operations: When leadership is too involved in daily tasks instead of strategic planning, it's time to scale. Shifting the focus to high-level initiatives is crucial for growth.

How to Scale a Business

Scaling a business is challenging but essential for long-term success. Here's a step-by-step guide to grow your company effectively:

Define your objectives:

Establish clear, specific goals for growth. Break down long-term objectives into actionable, measurable steps that guide your efforts and align your team.

Optimize processes:

Streamline your operations to improve efficiency. Identify and eliminate redundant tasks, automate them where possible, and continuously refine your processes to handle increased demand.

Broaden your market:

Reach new customers by expanding into new markets or segments. Conduct market research to understand your target audience and develop tailored marketing strategies to attract them.

Strengthen your team:

Build a capable and cohesive team. Hire individuals who align with your company's values and goals. Invest in their development through training and team-building activities.

Form strategic alliances:

Collaborate with other businesses to access new markets, resources, and expertise. Seek partnerships that complement your strengths and create mutually beneficial opportunities.

Leverage technology:

Adopt new technologies to enhance your business operations. Use tools that automate routine tasks, improve productivity, and provide valuable data insights to drive decision-making.

Track performance:

Implement KPIs to measure your progress. Regularly review these metrics to identify areas for improvement and adjust your strategies accordingly.

Maintain customer connections:

Prioritize customer satisfaction by actively seeking feedback and addressing their needs. Foster loyalty through excellent service and engagement, turning customers into repeat buyers and advocates.

Continuously innovate:

Embrace a culture of continuous improvement. Regularly assess your products and services, encourage creative thinking, and be willing to take calculated risks to stay ahead of the competition.

Leveraging Technology for Business Growth

Technology offers numerous ways for businesses to enhance efficiency and drive growth. Here are key strategies to leverage technology effectively:

Automate financial operations:

Use cloud-based accounting tools to automate financial functions. Solutions like Xero provide live access to financial data, digital invoicing, and real-time bank integration, making financial management simpler and more accurate.

Monitor cash flow in real-time:

Implement tools that provide live cash flow management. Applications like MyCashFlowApp offer daily forecasts, helping you anticipate and manage cash shortages well in advance.

Enhance KPI tracking:

Utilize cloud dashboards to track and improve KPIs. Integrated systems allow you to monitor live sales, payroll, and financial data, facilitating precise performance tracking and strategic adjustments.

Increase brand visibility on social media:

Leverage social media platforms to build brand awareness. Tools like Hootsuite can schedule posts across multiple channels, track engagement analytics, and enhance your social media marketing efforts.

Strengthen company culture with cloud solutions:

Use cloud tools to build and maintain a positive company culture. Platforms like Office Vibe collect employee feedback, while recognition tools like Hi5 encourage peer appreciation, fostering a supportive work environment.

Optimize lead generation and sales:

Adopt Customer Relationship Management (CRM) systems to streamline lead generation and sales processes. Tools like Salesforce and HubSpot automate tracking leads and sales activities, ensuring no potential business opportunities are overlooked.

By integrating these technologies, businesses can enhance productivity, improve financial oversight, and foster stronger relationships with customers and employees, ultimately driving sustainable growth.

Effective Hiring Strategies

As your business grows, hiring and managing a team effectively is crucial. Here are key strategies:

Strengthen company culture:

A strong, supportive culture attracts and retains skilled workers. Positive online employee job satisfaction reviews enhance your employer's brand, differentiating you from competitors. Improve workplace culture with effective onboarding and opportunities for growth.

Streamline hiring:

Create clear job descriptions, automate tasks with applicant tracking systems, and set clear hiring timelines. This ensures a quick, efficient process that attracts top candidates.

Encourage employee referrals:

Implement an employee referral program with incentives like bonuses or extra vacation days. Employees can identify and refer high-quality candidates, lowering recruitment costs and improving retention rates.

Write clear job postings:

Craft detailed job postings with clear expectations, required skills, and qualifications. Highlight your company's unique aspects and benefits to attract the right candidates. Include an equal opportunity statement to show your commitment to diversity.

Define candidate criteria:

Set specific minimum qualifications to filter out unfit candidates quickly, saving time and ensuring only qualified candidates proceed.

Standardize the hiring process:

Align all stakeholders on job requirements, screening criteria, and evaluation methods to reduce bias and improve efficiency. This ensures fair hiring practices and a smooth process.

Use social media:

Utilize LinkedIn and other platforms to find candidates. Use relevant hashtags, join industry groups, and use advanced search options to connect with a broader pool of qualified candidates.

Engage passive candidates:

Target candidates who are currently employed but not actively seeking new opportunities. Enhance your online presence and employer branding to attract these individuals, expanding your candidate pool to include unique, highly skilled individuals.

When implementing these strategies, entrepreneurs build a strong, efficient, and motivated team to drive business growth.

Team Management Strategies

Communicate openly and transparently:

Keep your team informed about company and team goals, tasks, and deadlines. Share your tasks and problem-solving approaches to foster collaboration and accountability. This builds trust, motivates innovation, and allows for quick problem resolution.

Set clear team goals:

Define and communicate specific, achievable team goals to focus efforts and minimize distractions. Use tools to track progress and ensure all tasks align with these objectives.

Provide regular feedback:

Offer constructive feedback regularly to guide improvement and boost morale. Listen to your team's feedback, provide necessary resources, and make the work environment supportive. Frequent feedback sessions help improve performance and trust.

Delegate tasks:

Assign tasks based on team members' skills and experience. Trust their capabilities, avoid overloading them, and use

274 M. A. GALLANT

274

M. A. GALLANT

management tools to monitor progress and balance workloads effectively.

Manage time efficiently:

Prioritize tasks and plan time allocation accurately to reduce stress and increase productivity. Use historical data and time-tracking tools to make precise time estimates and promptly address inefficiencies.

Settle team issues:

Address performance or behavior issues promptly and constructively. Use structured templates to outline problems, root causes, and solutions. Document discussions and corrective steps to ensure clarity and accountability.

Hire effectively and efficiently:

Integrate new hires smoothly through effective onboarding. Introduce them to the team, company culture, and necessary tools. A thorough onboarding process enhances employee retention and productivity.

Create a positive team culture:

Foster a supportive and collaborative work environment. Recognize achievements, encourage teamwork, and promote a healthy work-life balance to keep morale high and retain top talent.

By implementing these strategies, managers can build a cohesive, efficient, and motivated team, driving overall business success.

Overcoming Challenges

Avoid hiring mistakes:

Selecting the wrong employees can hinder growth. Focus on hiring skilled and culturally fit candidates to build a strong team.

Manage cash flow:

Scaling requires a significant upfront investment, straining cash flow. Plan ahead, create detailed budgets, and consider external funding options to maintain financial stability.

Compete beyond price:

Competing solely on price can erode margins. Differentiate your business through quality, innovation, and exceptional customer service.

Preserve company culture:

Rapid growth can dilute your culture. Prioritize cultural integration through clear values, strong leadership, and consistent communication to maintain a cohesive work environment.

Attract new customers:

Expanding your customer base is crucial. Implement targeted marketing strategies, leverage customer referrals, and continuously improve your offerings to attract and retain customers.

Develop efficient processes:

Thoughtful processes and operations are essential for scalability. Streamline workflows, automate tasks, and establish clear procedures to enhance efficiency and productivity.

Innovate your products:

Continuously improving and developing your products keeps your business competitive. Invest in research and development to meet evolving customer needs and market demands.

Build a solid team:

Establish a competent and motivated team. Invest in training and development, promote from within, and create a supportive work environment to foster growth and loyalty.

Prepare for growth:

Strategically prepare your business for expansion. Assess your infrastructure, systems scalability, and market opportunities to ensure readiness for growth.

Summary

This chapter provides practical insights and strategies to help you navigate the challenges of scaling your business and achieving sustained growth. Key takeaways include avoiding hiring mistakes, managing cash flow effectively, competing beyond price, preserving company culture, attracting new customers, developing efficient processes, innovating your products, building a solid team, and preparing strategically for growth.

The next chapter explores balancing the demands of education and entrepreneurship. This upcoming discussion will provide essential strategies for young entrepreneurs to succeed in both their academic and business pursuits. Stay tuned to discover how to manage your time, leverage resources, and maintain a balance between school and your entrepreneurial ambitions.

Chapter 11
Balancing Business and Education

The key is not to prioritize what's on your schedule,
but to schedule your priorities.

–Stephen Covey

T HIS QUOTE ABOVE HIGHLIGHTS a crucial aspect of balancing multiple responsibilities: organizing your priorities rather than merely managing your tasks. For teen entrepreneurs, this principle is especially vital. Juggling the demands of school and running a business can be overwhelming, but success in both areas is possible with the right strategies.

In this chapter, I jump into essential tactics to balance the demands of education and entrepreneurship. You will learn how to manage your time efficiently, set clear priorities, leverage resources, and keep a healthy balance between your academic and entrepreneurial pursuits. Adopting these techniques ensures that neither your studies nor your business suffers, and allows you to excel in both.

The Importance of Work-Life Balance

Work-life balance is essential for a healthy and productive life. Successfully balancing professional and personal responsibilities ensures you can handle both without becoming stressed or overwhelmed. Understanding why work-life balance is vital helps you manage negative emotions and develop effective time-management strategies. Here's why maintaining this balance is crucial:

Benefits of a healthy work-life balance

Boosted productivity:

Achieving a balance between work and life leads to increased productivity. When you allocate time efficiently, you focus better on your tasks, leading to higher-quality work and greater output.

Enhanced time management:

Balancing work and personal life improves your time management skills. Prioritizing tasks and setting boundaries ensures that neither your professional nor personal life suffers.

Improved physical and mental health:

Maintaining a healthy work-life balance supports both physical and mental well-being. Regular exercise, adequate sleep, and leisure activities reduce stress and enhance overall health, keeping you energetic and focused.

Reduced absenteeism:

A balanced lifestyle reduces sickness and absenteeism. Employees who manage stress and maintain good health are less likely to take sick days, providing consistent productivity.

Happier and less stressed workforce:

Employees who achieve work-life balance are generally happier and less stressed. This positive mindset contributes to a more pleasant and productive work environment.

Valuing personal and family life:

Balancing work and personal life shows employees that their free time and family lives matter. This recognition fosters a supportive and inclusive work culture.

Engaged and valued employees:

Employees who feel their personal life is respected are more engaged and motivated. They feel valued by their employer, which boosts morale and loyalty.

Prioritizing work-life balance creates a healthier, more productive, and more fulfilling lifestyle. Understanding and implementing these strategies helps you achieve balance, leading to personal and professional success.

Managing Your Time Effectively

Effective time management is crucial for entrepreneurs. Amid the excitement of launching a new venture, it's easy to become overwhelmed with tasks, risking productivity and personal well-being. Mastering time management enhances productivity, reduces stress, and maintains a healthy work-life balance. Let's explore why time management is vital for entrepreneurs. Allow me to provide practical tips to help manage your time efficiently:

Why is time management important?

Less stress:

Effective time management helps reduce stress by allowing you to plan and prioritize your tasks. With a clear schedule, you can manage your workload without feeling overwhelmed.

Eliminate distractions:

By organizing your time, you minimize distractions. Setting specific times for checking emails or social media helps you stay focused on important tasks.

Prioritize tasks:

Time management enables you to prioritize tasks, ensuring that you focus on what's most important first. This leads to better outcomes and more efficient use of your time.

Boost productivity:

Properly managing your time increases productivity. By allocating specific time blocks to tasks, you can work more efficiently and achieve more in less time.

Become more efficient:

Efficiency improves when you manage your time well. Streamlined workflows and organized schedules mean you accomplish tasks more quickly and accurately.

Better decision-making:

With effective time management, you can make better decisions. When you're not rushing, you have the mental space to consider options thoroughly and choose the best course of action.

Planning:

Planning is a core component of time management. Creating detailed plans and schedules ensures all necessary tasks are accounted for and deadlines are met.

Setting realistic goals:

Setting realistic goals is crucial for effective time management. Break down larger objectives into smaller, manageable tasks with achievable deadlines to stay motivated and on track.

Taking breaks:

Incorporating breaks into your schedule is essential. Regular breaks help maintain your mental and physical health, keeping you refreshed and productive.

Time Management Strategies for Busy Entrepreneurs

Entrepreneurship requires top-notch time management skills. Here are key strategies tailored for busy entrepreneurs:

- **Set clear goals and prioritize tasks**: Define achievable goals and prioritize tasks based on urgency and importance.

- **Plan and schedule your day**: Craft a daily schedule, allocating time for tasks and allowing for interruptions.

- **Learn to delegate**: Empower your team by delegating tasks that others can handle efficiently.

- **Embrace the two-minute rule**: Tackle quick tasks immediately to prevent them from piling up.

- **Practice the Pomodoro technique**: Break work into intervals with short breaks to maintain focus and prevent burnout.

- **Avoid multitasking**: Focus on one task at a time to optimize efficiency and workflow.

- **Limit distractions**: Identify and minimize distractions to create a conducive work environment.

Incorporating these strategies will enhance productivity and propel your business forward.

First Things First

Prioritizing tasks is essential for entrepreneurs facing tight schedules. This is a process of organizing your to-do list based on urgency and importance. It ensures efficient time management, reduces stress, and maintains work-life balance.

Proven prioritization technique

Compile a master task list by gathering all tasks in one place to assess and prioritize effectively. Distinguish between tasks that demand immediate attention and those contributing to long-term goals. Identify tasks that can be automated or delegated to streamline workflow. Lastly, minimize interruptions and focus on high-priority tasks to enhance productivity.

Tackle tasks that are labeled for immediate attention as soon as possible. Next, consider how to automate or delegate other items on your list and implement those actions. Any tasks that don't meet these criteria should be handled next. Finally, schedule time each week to work on tasks related to long-term goals.

- Pro Tip: Place your cell phone in another room while working on your to-do list. This means you won't be tempted to check every notification alert.

By implementing these strategies, entrepreneurs can optimize their time and achieve business success.

Task Management Tools for Entrepreneurs

Discover the top task prioritization tools for entrepreneurs:

- **ClickUp**: Utilize ClickUp's Priority Matrix Template to determine your next steps efficiently. ClickUp streamlines task organization and collaboration, catering to teams focused on productivity and results.

- **ProductPlan**: Prioritize tasks swiftly with ProductPlan's intuitive interface. This software enables teams to create detailed product roadmaps, ensuring clarity and alignment.

- **Scoro**: Optimize time management with Scoro's comprehensive work management features. Track projects, analyze profitability, and automate tasks to enhance productivity.

- **Reveall**: Reveall facilitates product discovery and prioritization with its scoring system. Teams can prioritize tasks effectively and track outcomes alongside product goals.

- **Productboard**: Customize prioritization formulas with Productboard to align with your objectives.

Organize product features efficiently and prioritize tasks based on customer insights.

- **airfocus**: Identify and prioritize critical tasks with airfocus's prioritization model. This platform aids decision-making by considering customer feedback and strategic goals.

- **Aha!**: Build visual product roadmaps and streamline workflows with Aha!. Prioritize tasks based on product value scores and integrate customer insights seamlessly.

- **Craft.io**: Plan effective product release cycles with Craft.io's flexible prioritization features. Utilize various prioritization types and formula builders to manage tasks efficiently.

- **Google Keep**: Keep track of tasks and priorities effortlessly with Google Keep. While lightweight, it offers a user-friendly interface for task prioritization and note-taking.

- **Evernote Teams**: Collaborate seamlessly and share prioritization processes with Evernote Teams. Although primarily a note-taking app, it can serve as a lightweight project planning and prioritization tool.

Prioritize Yourself

Entrepreneurial burnout, a consequence of relentless work, is a serious concern for business owners. Despite the demands of running a business, it's crucial to prioritize self-care to avoid burnout. Here's why and how:

What is entrepreneurial burnout?

Entrepreneurial burnout is the exhaustion of one's mental, physical, and emotional well-being due to chronic stress from continuous work. Lack of recognition, the drive to push forward, and constant overworking contribute to burnout.

Signs and symptoms of burnout

- Chronic exhaustion, difficulty getting out of bed, or staying awake

- Physical ailments like fainting or collapse due to prolonged stress

- Low productivity, motivation, efficacy, and focus

- Feelings of inefficacy, detachment, or negative thoughts about work

- Emotional changes like irritability, cynicism, or mood swings

- Mental illnesses such as depression, anxiety, or psychological stress

How to avoid entrepreneurial burnout

Rely on others:

Delegate tasks to employees, agencies, or freelancers to lighten your workload. Seek support from VA sites, job postings, or friends and family.

Unplug once a week:

Disconnect from work-related technology to recharge and reduce stress. Research shows that unplugging increases satisfaction and productivity.

Create your schedule:

Set boundaries by scheduling work hours and leaving weekends free. Establishing a routine fosters focus and work-life balance.

Change your routine:

Work from different locations to avoid monotony and boost creativity. Spend time outdoors or in new environments to rejuvenate your mind.

Care for yourself:

Prioritize health with nutritious meals and adequate sleep. Aim for at least seven hours of quality sleep per night to support well-being.

Build your network:

Surround yourself with supportive entrepreneurs to share experiences and advice. Join local business groups, find mentors, and engage with the community.

Get some exercise:

Incorporate regular exercise into your routine to reduce stress and improve your mood. Aim for at least 30 minutes of activity daily, such as walking, jogging, or joining fitness classes.

Prioritizing self-care is essential for sustaining long-term success and well-being as an entrepreneur. Implement these tips to protect yourself from burnout and thrive in both your personal and professional life.

The Power of Seeking Support

As an entrepreneur, seeking support is not a sign of weakness but a strategic move essential for building a successful business. Here's why and how to ask for help. Reasons asking for help as an entrepreneur is essential:

You're spending time learning to do a task yourself.

- Time spent learning tasks like web design or writing detracts from your focus on your business vision.

- Hiring freelancers for specialized tasks saves time and ensures professional results.

Managing your finances is eating away at your work-week.

- Juggling day-to-day finances consumes valuable time and focus.

- Partnering with trusted advisors like PNC Business Banking streamlines financial management, freeing up time for strategic decisions.

You're constantly putting out fires.

- Entrepreneurship brings new challenges daily, but having support systems in place prevents burnout and maintains productivity.

- Virtual assistants or productivity coaches can help manage unexpected tasks and optimize workflow.

It feels like you're sitting on a mountain of menial tasks.

- Handling all tasks yourself drains energy and detracts from strategic planning.

- Delegating menial tasks allows you to focus on high-impact activities and decision-making.

You look at other businesses and wonder: How'd they do that?

- Many successful businesses delegate tasks to experts to maintain quality and efficiency.

- Seeking help when overwhelmed by specific tasks lets you focus on leading and growing your business.

Exploring various support options and asking for help when needed is crucial for maintaining focus, efficiency, and mental well-being.

Effective Ways to Ask for Help as an Entrepreneur

Don't think of help as a debt

Rather than seeing asking for help as a burden, embrace it as a fundamental aspect of business relationships. Utilizing existing networks and seeking assistance fosters connections and expands your circle of support.

Play ignorant

Embrace your lack of knowledge in certain areas as an opportunity to seek innovative solutions. Asking questions without feeling a need to appear knowledgeable can lead to unexpected breakthroughs.

Know what you need help with

Identify specific areas where you require assistance before seeking help. A clear understanding of your needs enables you to ask targeted questions and receive relevant advice promptly.

Show that they're the right person to help

Research potential helpers and demonstrate why they are suited to assist. Making a compelling case for why a particular individual can help increase the likelihood of receiving valuable support.

Do the legwork

Make it easy for your helper by providing the necessary information and context. Simplifying the process for your helper, such as by providing relevant details in your request, increases the likelihood of receiving assistance.

Be grateful

Express gratitude to those who offer help through verbal appreciation or gestures. Showing appreciation acknowledges the assistance received and strengthens the relationship with your helper.

Walking in Their Shoes

Richard Branson starts his day with exercise

- The billionaire entrepreneur begins his day with a workout at 5 a.m., which he believes enhances his productivity significantly. Incorporating physical activity into his morning routine allows him to optimize his mental clarity and performance throughout the day.

Marcus Lemonis creates "knockout lists"

- Lemonis compiles a list of five tasks he aims to accomplish each day, ensuring their completion without exception. By setting clear priorities and focusing on essential tasks, Lemonis maximizes his productivity and maintains consistent progress.

Mary Callahan Erdoes emphasizes calendar management

- Erdoes underscores the importance of owning one's calendar to manage responsibilities and prioritize tasks. By proactively managing her schedule, Erdoes avoids being overwhelmed by competing demands and maintains organizational efficiency.

Daymond John maximizes his time creatively

- The "Shark Tank" investor delegates tasks, handles emails during travel, and optimizes personal interactions for efficiency. John adopts creative strategies to make the most of his time, allowing him to focus on high-impact activities and delegate routine tasks effectively.

Arianna Huffington advocates for taking breaks

- Huffington emphasizes the importance of pausing during the day, especially for meals, to recharge and reduce stress. Integrating breaks into her schedule enhances productivity and well-being, contributing to a more balanced and effective workday.

Tracy Anderson utilizes written notes for organization

- Anderson relies on written notes and visualizations to organize ideas and tasks, facilitating effective decision-making and planning. By leveraging physical notebooks, Anderson ensures clarity and coherence in managing responsibilities and projects.

By following these examples and implementing the strategies outlined in this book, you can master the art of balancing your educational and entrepreneurial pursuits. Remember, the key to success is not just hard work, but smart work. Prioritize your tasks, manage your time effectively, seek support when needed, and most importantly, take care of yourself. With these tools, you can achieve both academic and entrepreneurial success.

I sincerely thank you for choosing my book in your quest to become a young adult entrepreneur. Please reach out and share your story of business ownership with me. You can email Melissa@EtheriaPublishing.com

If this book has been valuable to you, I would greatly appreciate it if you could leave a review, sharing your thoughts with others who may benefit from this knowledge. Please scan the QR code to review on Amazon. I also welcome reviews on other websites or social media.

Please Scan to leave

Your Amazon Review

If you are reading this with Kindle please continue until prompted to leave a review.

Here's to your success as an entrepreneur! I'm cheering for you!

M. A. Gallant

Conclusion

THROUGHOUT THIS BOOK, WE'VE dove deep into the essence of entrepreneurship, uncovering the qualities, strategies, and mindsets that define success in the business world. From understanding the fundamentals of entrepreneurship to mastering essential skills like time management, market research, business planning, and financial management, you've been equipped with a comprehensive playbook to navigate the entrepreneurial landscape.

At its core, entrepreneurship is about resilience, determination, problem-solving, and empathy. It's about embracing challenges as opportunities, continuously learning and adapting, and staying true to your vision despite obstacles along the way. As we reflect on the journey we've taken together, it's clear that success in entrepreneurship is not merely about having a great idea but also about having the mindset and skills to turn that idea into reality.

As you move forward on your entrepreneurial journey, remember the stories of success we've explored and draw inspiration from them. Whether it's Richard Branson's dedication to fitness, Hillary Yip's business creation at age 12, or Tesla's devotion to innovation, each success story offers valuable lessons and insights you can apply to your own endeavors.

Now is the time to take action. Seize the opportunities that lie ahead and let your entrepreneurial spirit soar. The future is yours to create! Take the first step towards your dreams, knowing every great success story starts with a single decision to act.

As you continue your entrepreneurial journey, I encourage you to reflect on your experiences, learn from your failures and successes, and never lose sight of your vision.

References

Advantages and disadvantages of forming your business as a corporation. (n.d.). Indeed. https://www.indeed.com/hire/c/info/advantages-and-disadvantages-of-corporation

Aghadjanian, N. (2021, July 15). *Top reason consumers distrust a brand? Asking for too much information.* Alistdaily. https://www.alistdaily.com/strategy/jebbit-index-finds-interactive-experiences-increase-consumer-trust/

Azevedo, S. (2024, April 29). *How to improve your team management skills.* ClickUp. https://clickup.com/blog/team-management/

Barnardt, L. (2018, October 17). *7 ways to leverage technology to scale up your business.* LinkedIn. https://www.linkedin.com/pulse/7-ways-leverage-technology-scale-up-your-business-barnardt-ca-sa-

Benedict, C. (2023, November 16). *The beginner's guide to trade show marketing.* Constant Contact. https://www.constantcontact.com/blog/the-beginners-guide-to-trade-show-marketing/

Benefits of being a young entrepreneur. (2022, March 15). Entrepreneurship Campus. https://entrepreneurship.de/en/magazin/benefits-of-being-a-young-entrepreneur

Benefits of Search Engine Marketing (SEM). (2022, January 6). LinkedIn. https://www.linkedin.com/pulse/benefits-search-engine-marketing-sem-lead-generation

Berry, J. (n.d.). *7 tips to manage your business finances.* Lendingtree. https://www.lendingtree.com/business/managing-small-business-finances/

Boss business ideas to become your own. (n.d.). Intuit Mailchimp. https://mailchimp.com/resources/how-to-create-business-idea/

Bozigian, C. (2024, February 6). *Brand archetypes 101: How to choose one + top examples.* Digital Silk. https://www.digitalsilk.com/digital-trends/brand-archetypes/

Business structure. (n.d.). Corporate finance Institute. https://corporatefinanceinstitute.com/resources/management/business-structure/

Can a minor own a business? (n.d.). *Bizee.* https://bizee.com/blog/can-a-minor-own-a-business

Carter, J. (2023, March 7). *How to develop & nurture an entrepreneurial mindset?* DSers. https://www.dsers.com/blog/entrepreneurial-mindset/

Common mistakes by teen entrepreneurs. (n.d.). Teen Business. https://www.teenbusiness.com/mistakes-by-teen-entrepreneurs

Cox, M. (n.d.). *The complete guide to managing finances for your business.* First Bank. https://www.myfirst.bank/articles/the-complete-guide-to-managing-finances-for-your-business

Dewitt, K. (2024, May 6). *Partnership advantages and disadvantages.* Patriot. https://www.patriotsoftware.com/blog/accounting/pros-cons-business-partnership-advantages-disadvantages-questions/

Diane, F. (n.d.). *How to form a corporation in 11 steps.* Legal Zoom. https://www.legalzoom.com/articles/how-to-form-a-corporation

Dublino, J. (2023, November 30). *10 proven tips for young entrepreneurs to start off strong.* Business.com. https://www.business.com/articles/tips-for-young-entrepreneurs/

Ducker, C. (n.d.). *Why passion is essential to entrepreneurship and building a thriving business.* Youpreneur. https://youpreneur.com/why-passion-is-essential-to-entrepreneurship-and-building-a-thriving-business/#

Elkins, K. (2017, February 17). *14 time-management tricks from Richard Branson and other successful people.* CNBC.

https://www.cnbc.com/2017/02/17/time-management-t ricks-from-richard-branson-other-successful-people.html #

Entrepreneurial mindset - 10 most crucial characteristics 2024. (2024, April 25). Nexford University. https://ww w.nexford.edu/insights/entrepreneurial-mindset

Entrepreneurship for teens 101. (2023, September 21). Greenlight. https://greenlight.com/learning-center/earn ing/entrepreneurship-for-teens

Establishing and maintaining brand consistency. (n.d.). Intuit Mailchimp. https://mailchimp.com/resources/bra nd-consistency/#

8 traits of successful entrepreneurs--Do you have what it takes? (n.d.). Minority Business Development Agency. https://archive.mbda.gov/news/blog/2010/07/8-traits-s uccessful-entrepreneurs-do-you-have-what-it-takes.html

Fanaras, L. (2023, April 17). *The 5 key elements of a successful marketing strategy.* LinkedIn. https://www.linkedin.com/pulse/5-key-eleme nts-successful-marketing-strategy-linda-fanaras

Fligler, L. (2023, September 11). *Influence your way to success: 6 compelling benefits of collaborating with influencer marketing.* Yellowhead. https://www.yellowhead.com/bl og/benefits-of-influencer-marketing/

Flores, M. L. (2021, October 30). *Life lessons learned as a teen entrepreneur.* LinkedIn. https://www.linkedin.com/pulse/l ife-lessons-learned-teen-entrepreneur-melanie-l-flores

Fontalvo, C. (2024, April 9). *6 successful companies founded by teen entrepreneurs.* Leangap. https://www.leangap.org/artic les/6-successful-companies-founded-by-teen-entrepreneurs

Fontinelle, A. (2023, December 11). *16 tax deductions and benefits for the self-employed.* Investopedia. https://www.investopedia.com/articles/tax/09/self-em ployed-tax-deductions.asp

Foo, S. (2020, May 27). *37 inspiring branding quotes from billionaires & CEOs.* SpeechSilver. https://speechsilver.com /branding-quotes/

Freedman, M. (2023, August 31). *How to conduct a market analysis for your business.* Business News Daily. https://www.businessnewsdaily.com/15751-conduct-m arket-analysis.html

Freelance entrepreneurship: Turning your passion into profit. (2024, April 4). Faster Capital. https://fastercapital.com/content/Freelance-Entrepreneurs hip--Turning-Your-Passion-into-Profit.html#Turning-Your -Passion-into-Profit-Identifying-Your-Passion--Finding-Your -Niche

15 telling signs it's time to scale up your company. (2023, September 5). Forbes.

https://www.forbes.com/sites/forbesbusinesscouncil/20
23/09/05/15-telling-signs-its-time-to-scale-up-your-com
pany/?sh=138ffcac2f20

15+ best small business ideas for teens to easily start. (2023,
November 8.). EComposer. https://ecomposer.io/blogs/
case-studies/business-ideas-for-teens

5 reasons it's essential to ask for help. (2018, June 4). Entrepreneur. https://www.entrepreneur.com/business-ne
ws/5-reasons-its-essential-to-ask-for-help/312287

*5 types of business taxes (And why your
business structure matters).* (2022, July 6).
LinkedIn. https://www.linkedin.com/pulse/5-types-bus
iness-taxes-why-your-structure-matters-

Gale-coleman, E. (2020, May 5). *5 teenage entrepreneurs
on turning their passions to profit online.* The Teen Mag-
azine. https://www.theteenmagazine.com/5-teenage-ent
repreneurs-on-turning-their-passions-to-profit-online

Gargaro, D. (2017, February 17). *Make your brand more
credible to attract bigger and better clients.* LinkedIn.
https://www.linkedin.com/pulse/make-your-brand-more
-credible-attract-bigger-better-clients-gargaro

Getman, C. (n.d.). *The 16 marketing KPIs you should be
measuring (But probably aren't).* Vital. https://vitaldesig
n.com/16-marketing-kpis-to-measure/

Goldin, K. (2018, July 16). *6 ways to ask for help as an entrepreneur.* Forbes. https://www.forbes.com/sites/karagoldin/2018/07/16/6-w ays-to-ask-for-help-as-an-entrepreneur/?sh=7ee7cfbd26a5

Gordon, E. D. (2017, August 2). *5 challenges facing young entrepreneurs (and how to overcome them).* Goalcast. https://www.goalcast.com/5-challenges-that-face-you ng-entrepreneurs-and-how-to-overcome-them/

Grenier, L. (2023, November 17). *How to do market research in 4 steps: a lean approach to marketing research.* Hotjar. https://www.hotjar.com/blog/market-research/

Griswold, D. (2024, March 22). *What is an LLC? Definition and steps on how to form an LLC.* Wolter Kluwer. https://www.wolterskluwer.com/en/expert-insights/how-to -form-an-llc-what-is-an-llc-advantages-disadvantages-and-m ore

Guberti, M. (2015, November 4). *What it means to be a teenager entrepreneur.* Marc Guberti. https://marcguberti.c om/2015/11/what-it-means-to-be-a-teenager-entrepreneur/

Guinness, H. (2023, November 22). *The 6 best social media management tools in 2024.* Zapier. https://zapier.com/blog /best-social-media-management-tools/

Hargrave, M. (2024, January 11). *How to file small business taxes: A 7-step guide.* QuickBooks. https://quickbooks.intu it.com/r/taxes/file-small-business-taxes/

Hayes, A. (2024, January 25). *Business plan: What it is, what's included, and how to write one.* Investopedia. https://www.investopedia.com/terms/b/business-plan.asp#toc-common-elements-of-a-business-plan

Hendricks, D. (2023, October 27). *8 reasons business plans fail that no one wants to talk about.* Bplans. https://www.bplans.com/business-planning/tips/reasons-plans-fail/

How to create a business budget for your small business. (n.d.). Zoho. https://www.zoho.com/books/guides/how-to-create-a-realistic-business-budget.html

How to define brand identity in 11 Steps (and why it matters). (n.d.). Indeed. https://www.indeed.com/hire/c/info/brand-identity

How to find your target audience in 5 steps. (2023, September 25). Adobe Express. https://www.adobe.com/express/learn/blog/target-audience

How to raise money for a business: 11 sources of funding. (n.d.). Gofundme. https://www.gofundme.com/c/fundraising-ideas/business

Hu, W., Xu, Y., Zhao, F., & Chen, Y. (2022). Entrepreneurial passion and entrepreneurial success-The role of psychological capital and entrepreneurial policy support. *Frontiers in Psychology, 13,* 792066. https://doi.org/10.3389/fpsyg.2022.792066

Importance of networking for young entrepreneurs. (2023, April 27). TechDevAcademy. https://techdevacademy.com /importance-of-networking-for-young-entrepreneurs/

Improve your search engine rankings. (2024, April 9). Business. https://business.gov.au/online-and-digital/business-w ebsite/improve-your-search-engine-rankings

Iqbal, S. (2023, October 9). *Navigating legal contracts: An entrepreneur's guide to key business agreements.* Meduim. https://medium.com/@si5716490/navigating-legal-contract s-an-entrepreneurs-guide-to-key-business-agreements-399e4 d173180

K For entrepreneurs a comprehensive guide to saving money on taxes and investing wisely. (2024, April 21). FasterCapital. https://fastercapital.com/content/K-For-Entrepreneurs---A -Comprehensive-Guide-To-Saving-Money-On-Taxes-And-I nvesting-Wisely.html#

Kenan, J. (2023, June 13). *Brand voice: What it is and why it matters.* Sproutsocial. https://sproutsocial.com/insights/br and-voice/

Kimbarovsky, R. (2024, May 6). *10 game-changing tips for crafting an unbeatable business plan.* Crowspring. https://w ww.crowdspring.com/blog/business-plan-tips/#keep

Klesser, G. (n.d.). *Setting up your first paid search campaign.* The Online Advertising Guide. https://theonlineadvertisin gguide.com/paid-search-guide/first-paid-search-campaign/

Leist, R. (2024, April 4). *How to do keyword research for SEO: A beginner's guide.* Hubspot. https://blog.hubspot.com/marketing/how-to-do-keyword-research-ht#

Lewis, D. (2017, February 24). *Walk before you run: An interview with Benjamin Stern, the 17-year-old founder of Nohbo.* New Hope Network. https://www.newhope.com/business-management/walk-before-you-run-an-interview-with-benjamin-stern-the-17-year-old-founder-of-nohbo

Lewis, J. (2023, August 21). *Employee versus entrepreneurs mindset: What you need to know.* The Biz Foundary. https://thebizfoundry.org/2023/08/employee-versus-entrepreneur-mindset-what-you-need-to-know/#

Likarenko, Y. (2024, April 19). *How to build MVP: step-by-step guide.* Uptech. https://www.uptech.team/blog/build-an-mvp

Macready, H. (2022, November 7). *How to do social media marketing for small business.* Hootsuite. https://blog.hootsuite.com/social-media-tips-for-small-business-owners/

Marker, A. (2020, August 12). *Free small business budget templates.* Smartsheet. https://www.smartsheet.com/content/small-business-budget-templates

Mastering time management: Strategies for busy entrepreneurs. (2023, August 22). Adapting Social. https://adaptingsocial.com/entrepreneur-time-management/

Mathias, C. (n.d.). *How to form a partnership.* Nolo. https://www.nolo.com/legal-encyclopedia/50-state-guide-establishing-general-partnership.html

Milender, C. (n.d.). *40 inspiring work-life balance quotes to learn from.* Goskills. https://www.goskills.com/Office-Productivity/Resources/Work-life-balance-quotes

Nagle, C. (2023, April 30). *7 budgeting basics for small business owners.* Score. https://www.score.org/resource/blog-post/7-budgeting-basics-small-business-owners

Naqvi, A. (n.d.). *The importance of online presence for business.* Xavour. https://www.xavor.com/blog/the-importance-of-online-presence-for-business/

Nawaz, H. R. (2023, March 31). *Scaling your business: Overcoming challenges and strategies for successful expansion.* LinkedIn. https://www.linkedin.com/pulse/scaling-your-business-overcoming-challenges-expansion-hamid-rab-nawaz

Newberry, C., & Kwok, E. (2023, October 25). *Influencer marketing guide: How to work with influencers.* Hootsuite. https://blog.hootsuite.com/influencer-marketing/

Nikotina, A. (2016). *Employment vs entrepreneurship: Choosing the right path.* Ashton. https://www.ashtoncollege.ca/employee-entrepreneur-career-path/

Nine reasons why you need a business plan. (n.d.). Chase for Business. https://www.chase.com/business/knowledge-cen ter/start/reasons-for-business-plan

Odjick, D. (2023, December 15). *How to write a business plan in 9 steps (2024).* Shopify. https://www.shopify.com/blog/b usiness-plan

Ooijen, G. (2023, February 13). *How to scale a business in 9 steps.* Scribe. https://scribehow.com/library/how-to-scale -a-business

Partnership. (n.d.). *Partnership.* CFI. https://corporatefina nceinstitute.com/resources/management/partnership/

Patel, S. (2024, April 8). *A complete guide to successful brand positioning.* Hubspot. https://blog.hubspot.com/sales/bra nd-positioning-strategy#whatisbrandpositioning

Pitching business ideas: How to pitch your idea to investors. (2023, September 25). Indeed. https://www.indeed.com/ca reer-advice/career-development/pitching-business-ideas

Pooriya, K. (2023, March 2). *7 essential steps for crafting a winning marketing strategy.* LinkedIn. https://www.linkedin.com/pulse/7-essential-ste ps-crafting-winning-marketing-strategy-khorshidi

Post, J. (2024, May 15). *Time crunch: An entrepreneur's guide to prioritizing your tasks.* Business.com. https://www.busin ess.com/articles/entrepreneur-prioritize-tasks/

Puharich, R. (2022, February 16). *How to start a business as a teenager with no money.* Teen Learner. https://teenle arner.com/start-a-business-as-a-teenager-with-no-money/

Qayum, A. (2022, July 2). *How to avoid burnout: A guide for entrepreneurs.* OBERLO. https://www.oberlo.com/b log/how-to-avoid-burnout

Quote by Antoine de Saint-Exupéry. (n.d.) . Goodreads. https://www.goodreads.com/quotes/8747 6-a-goal-without-a-plan-is-just-a-wish

Quote by Daniel Lapin. (n.d.). Quote Fancy. https://quotefancy.com/quote/2324108/Daniel-Lapin -Give-your-due-diligence-to-understanding-business-or-y ou-will-have-no-place

Quote by Kamaran Ihsan Salih (n.d.). Quotefan-cy. https://quotefancy.com/quote/2043631/Kamaran-I hsan-Salih-Do-a-bit-research-before-you-plan

Quote by Madam C. J. Walker. (n.d.). Goodreads. https://www.goodreads.com/quotes/6565023-don-t-sit -down-and-wait-for-the-opportunities-to-come

Quote by Soledad O'Brien. (n.d.). Brainy Quote. https:// www.brainyquote.com/quotes/soledad_obrien_648638

Quote by Tony Hsieh. (n.d.). Quote Fancy. https://quotefancy.com/quote/757033/Tony-Hsieh-Chase

-the-vision-not-the-money-The-money-will-end-up-following-you

Rai, H. (n.d.). *17 inspirational startup quotes.* Startupxs. https://startupxs.com/quotes-startups/

Reddigari, M. (2019, May 7). *15 basic business terms every entrepreneur should learn.* Mile IQ. https://mileiq.com/blog/basic-business-terms

Smith, A. (2022, September 23). *A how-to guide for creating a business budget.* Bench. https://www.bench.co/blog/accounting/business-budget

Soni, A. (2024, January 16). *10 best income tax saving tips for an entrepreneur.* Tax2win. https://tax2win.in/guide/tax-saving-tips-for-entrepreneur

Stinson, N. (2017, September 5). *7 common myths about following your passion.* Chopra. https://chopra.com/blogs/personal-growth/7-common-myths-about-following-your-passion

Sutevski, D. (n.d.). *Why passion is your most valuable business asset and how to find about what you are passionate.* Entrepreneurship in a Box. https://www.entrepreneurshipinabox.com/870/find-what-are-you-passionate/

Sydney, B. (2023, February 27). *5 reasons having an online presence is essential in today's modern business world.*

LinkedIn. https://www.linkedin.com/pulse/5-reasons-havi
ng-online-presence-essential-todays-modern-barnwell

7 examples of entrepreneurial thinking in action. (2021,
March 15). VentureLab. https://venturelab.org/7-examples
-entrepreneurial-thinking-in-action/

The entrepreneurial mindset. (n.d.). Nfte. https://nfte.com
/entrepreneurial-mindset/#

The importance of mentorship for young entrepreneurs. (n.d.).
Friends of Puerto Rico. https://www.friendsofpuertorico.o
rg/blog/mentorship-for-young-entrepreneurs

The importance of time management for entrepreneurs. (2024,
May 27). *AIContentfy.* https://aicontentfy.com/en/blog/im
portance-of-time-management-for-entrepreneurs

*The importance of tracking your marketing
KPIs to make smarter decisions.* (n.d.). *InCon-
cert.* https://blog.inconcertcc.com/en/the-importance-of-tr
acking-your-marketing-kpis-to-make-smarter-decisions/

The importance of visual elements in your brand strategy. (n
.d.). Duct Tape. https://ducttapemarketing.com/visual-bra
nd-strategy/

*The power of entrepreneurship: Famous suc-
cess stories.* (2022, October 15). University of
Bolton. https://www.bolton.ac.uk/blogs/the-power-of-ent
repreneurship-famous-success-stories

The power of passion why you need it to succeed in startups. (2024, April 17). Faster Capital. https://fastercapital.com/content/The-Power-of-Passion--Why-You-Need-It-to-Succeed-in-Startups.html#How-to-Develop-Passion-for-Your-Startup-

To work with PDF tools was just. (n.d.). SmallPDF. https://smallpdf.online

Top 4 benefits of having an online presence for your business. (n.d.). Exeedcollege. https://exeedcollege.com/blog/top-4-benefits-of-having-an-online-presence-for-your-business/

Twin, A. (2024, February 24). *How to do market research, types, and example.* Investopedia. https://www.investopedia.com/terms/m/market-research.asp

10 best practices for hiring the right employees. (2023, June 8.). Upwork. https://www.upwork.com/resources/best-practices-for-hiring-employees#consider-passive-candidates

10 best work prioritization tools in 2024. (2024, May 13). ClickUp. https://clickup.com/blog/prioritization-tools/

10 common mistakes to avoid when building your digital marketing strategy. (2023, June 3). LinkedIn. https://www.linkedin.com/pulse/10-common-mistakes-avoid-when-building-your-digital-tech-solutions

365 marketing quotes to keep you fired up all year. (2020, October 2). Skyword. https://www.skyword.com/contents tandard/marketing-quotes/

Ward, S. (2022, September 13). *How to come up with a business idea.* The Balance. https://www.thebalancemoney.com/cre ate-winning-business-ideas-2947249

West, C. (2022, November 29). *What is email marketing? Your 101 guide to email campaigns.* Sproutsocial. https://s proutsocial.com/insights/email-marketing/

What is a sole proprietorship and how to start one. (2022, December 2.). Wolters Kluwer. https://www.wolterskluwer.com/en/expert-insights/wh at-is-a-sole-proprietorship-and-how-to-start-one#

Whatman, P. (2024, January 11). *Growth vs scaling: What's the difference and why does it matter?.* Spendesk. https://w ww.spendesk.com/en-eu/blog/growth-vs-scaling/

Why is an entrepreneurial mindset important for you? (2024, April 25). LinkedIn. https://www.linkedin.com/advice/0/why-entrep reneurial-mindset-important-you-skills-entrepreneurship#

Why work-life balance is important (With benefits and steps). (2023, August 31). Indeed. https://ca.indeed.com/career-advice/career-developm ent/why-work-life-balance-is-important

Why young entrepreneurs need mentors. (2021, February 9). Servecorp. https://www.servcorp.com.au/en/blog/business-networking/why-young-entrepreneurs-need-mentors/

Wirth, K. (2024, January 5). *How to come up with a good business idea.* Bplans. https://www.bplans.com/start-a-business/ideas/

Zerkalenkov, Z. (2024, January 8). *Brand identity: What it is and how to create a strong one.* Semrush. https://www.semrush.com/blog/build-brand-identity/

Zhukova, N. (2023, April 21). *How to create your buyer personas: the what, the why, and the how.* Semrush. https://www.semrush.com/blog/buyer-persona/#how-do-you-do-buyer-persona-research